Airliners in Flight

Nicholas A. Veronico and George Hall

MBI Publishing Company

First published in 1997 by MBI Publishing Company, 729 Prospect Avenue, PO Box 1, Osceola, WI 54020-0001 USA

MBI Publishing Company books are also available at discounts in bulk quantity for industrial or sales-promotional use. For details write to Special Sales Manager at Motorbooks International Wholesalers & Distributors, 729 Prospect Avenue, PO Box 1,Osceola, WI 54020-0001 USA.

Library of Congress Cataloging-in-Publication Data

Veronico, Nick
  Airliners in flight : a gallery of air-to-air photography / Nicholas A. Veronico and George Hall.
     p.   cm.
  Includes index.
  ISBN 0-7603-0215-4
  1. Transport planes. 2. Aeronautics, Commercial. 3. Photography of airplanes. I. Hall, George. II. Title.
TL685.4.V47   1997
629.133'340423—dc21   97-30404

On the front cover: One of the most photographed landmarks in the United States also makes a great back-drop for an airline commercial. Here a Continental 747 passes over San Francisco's Golden Gate Bridge. George Hall/Check Six

On the frontispiece: It is hard enough to fly formation with the Lear Jet and a subject aircraft. Multiply the difficulties by three when two Condor 767-330 (ER [extended range]) jetliners are led by a Boeing 757-230 during a June 1991 photo shoot. This was one of the hardest shoots for George Hall. Each aircraft must be spaced perfectly, as evidenced here. George Hall/Check Six

On the title page: Some of the photos that are delivered to the customer airlines are taken over famous landmarks, in this case the Sydney Harbor and Opera House. Clay Lacy ferried his camera-equipped Lear to Australia specifically for this shoot. George Hall/Check Six

On the back cover, top: Once a positive rate of climb has been established, the gear is retracted. This takeoff photograph was arranged by the airline for George Hall's cameras at Mojave, California. George Hall/Check Six

On the back cover, bottom: Japan Airlines Boeing 777-246 JA8981 (msn 27364) passes Washington State's Mt. Rainier. George Hall/Check Six

Edited by Mike Haenggi
Designed by Katie Finney

Printed in Hong Kong

CONTENTS

CHAPTER 1

THE MAKING OF A JETLINER

The Douglas Aircraft Company, a division of aerospace giant McDonnell Douglas Corporation, has delivered more than 45,000 aircraft since its inception in 1920. The company's designs are legendary—Douglas's DC-3 was the first economically viable and most widely used all-metal, twin-engine airliner, dominating the commercial airways from 1935 to 1945. The DC-4, -6, and -7 carried the company banner through the decade of the 1950s up to the jet age. Douglas's first commercial jet transport, the DC-8, flew on May 30, 1958. Seven years later, the manufacturer's most successful commercial jet design, the twin-engine DC-9, took off on its maiden flight on February 25, 1965.

Improvements to the DC-9 and, after the merger with McDonnell, the later MD series of twin-jets, has made Douglas a dominant force in the short-to-medium-range-air-

ABOVE: The Douglas Aircraft Company division of aerospace conglomerate McDonnell Douglas celebrated its 75th year of production in 1995. *McDonnell Douglas*

Korean Air and American Airlines DC-10s near completion. *Sam Sargent/Check Six*

liner market. The DC-9's first, or launch, customer was Delta Air Lines. Nearly 30 years later, Delta has once again become the launch customer for the improved MD-90 series—based on the original DC-9 design.

The aircraft are assembled at the company's 7-million-square-foot facility at Long Beach, California, that employs 10,000–11,000 people in its commercial aircraft division. McDonnell Douglas also builds the US Air Force's C-17 Globemaster III on the field.

To Sell an Airliner, the Manufacturer's Team Must Be in Place

The selling of commercial airliners is a never-ending process that eventually comes full circle. One of the most important elements is a continuing dialog between the manufacturer and the airlines of the world. The manufacturer must always try to stay abreast of the airline's needs and wants while trying to keep the airlines advised about what can be offered in terms of current aircraft designs incorporating today's and tomorrow's technology. This is accomplished through a variety of approaches. Product-support field-service representatives live with airline maintenance staff and operations people day in and day out at all of the major airports of the world. Many times, the product-support field staff maintains an office in an airline's hangar. That relationship keeps the manufacturer up to speed on how its present airliners are performing in the fleet. This also serves as a channel for keeping an airline's maintenance and

The second MD-90 awaiting installation of its two International Aero Engines V2500 powerplants. *McDonnell Douglas*

Douglas has a "product display area" that features full-size mock-ups of its products. This area is the closest in comparison to an automobile dealer's showroom. Here the new MD-90's cabin mock-up gives airline customers the opportunity to inspect the fuselage interior's appointments, including large overhead storage bins for carry-on luggage (with built-in hand rails to support passengers walking the aisle), indirect cabin lighting, and five-abreast seating. *McDonnell Douglas*

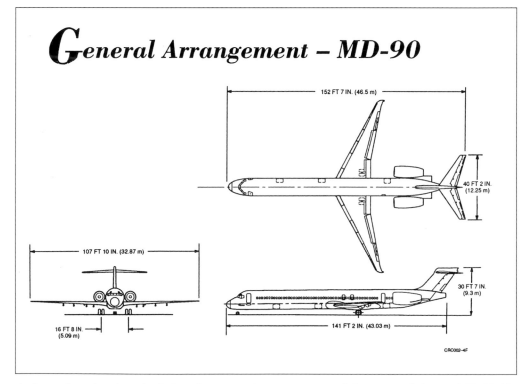

A three-view drawing depicting the general arrangement of the state-of-the-art MD-90-30. *McDonnell Douglas*

operations divisions informed on what the manufacturer is doing in terms of new airplanes and modifications to present designs.

The manufacturer's marketing staff works with its customers on a number of different levels. The market development department is staffed by people with engineering or airline backgrounds who are experts in all of the different facets of airline operations from route planning to economics and finance to maintenance and flight training. They stay in contact with the airlines, gathering information on each carrier and its trends, while at the same time disseminating information on the manufacturer's products and new developments. Douglas organizes its staff on a geographic basis—sections for the United States and the Americas, Europe, Middle East-Africa, and Asia-Pacific.

A department within marketing is dedicated entirely to airline/aircraft finance. This is a very important piece of the package when it comes time to negotiate price. This department helps the airlines develop a suitable financing package either for sale or lease. Whether a lease or outright purchase, each sale is different depending upon each airline's circumstances. Each manufacturer's finance staff can broker the lease arrangements or arrange financing through a number of sources.

Another segment of the marketing staff is responsible for continually reviewing and updating Douglas's economic and air-traffic forecasts, which are published every 12–15 months. From these studies, Douglas makes a prediction as to what the airlines' equipment needs will be over the next 10 and 20 years. This group looks at long term, while others within the organization look at the nearer term requirements of the airlines. These trend forecasts are another point of continuing dialog between the manufacturer and the airlines at their administrative and planning levels.

Douglas employs more than 10,000 workers at its Long Beach factory. MD-80- and MD-90-series aircraft are built on the same assembly line. Tri-jet MD-11s are constructed in the large buildings in the foreground. *McDonnell Douglas*

On September 30, 1996, McDonnell Douglas released its latest 20-year forecast. It estimated that the world's airlines, 457 in all, will need 13,600 new jetliners valued at $1.14 trillion. To meet this demand, Douglas predicts that 680 aircraft must be delivered per year through 2014, noting that at the end of 1995 a total of 1,859 aircraft were on order. Airline routes in the Asia Pacific corridor are expected to grow 8.1 percent annually, surpassing all North American-based airlines by 2013.

According to the McDonnell Douglas forecast, short-haul aircraft seating under 150 passengers will experience the largest segment of growth with an estimated 3,073 aircraft required. Airliners with only 100 seats used on short-haul routes will require 1,815 aircraft. The forecast also calls for 2,309 medium- and long-range 200-seaters; 2,142 medium- and long-range 300-seat planes; 1,803 medium- and long-range 400-seat airliners; and 543 aircraft capable of carrying 600 passengers over medium and long haul routes. The world's fleet of airliners will also double to 2,720 by the year 2014.

Sales representatives are organized on a geographic basis and will generally be assigned to sets of airlines within that area. It is their role to main-

The cockpit crew for the prototype MD-90's first flight were, from left, Flight Test Engineer Barry McCarthy, MD-90 Chief Test Pilot William Jones, and Test Pilot G. R. "Bear" Smith. *McDonnell Douglas*

sentatives as possible to come together on a host of issues —either looking at potential new models or discussing operational matters on aircraft in service. This keeps a manufacturer's products visible and the airlines aware that their hosts are customer and service oriented. That is a key part of the whole sales strategy.

Finally, company executives are continually traveling the world discussing Douglas's products with airline presidents and vice presidents.

Making the Sale

Having established a sales support team, the manufacturer begins to bring all of the puzzle pieces together. To make a sale, an aircraft builder must be on top of an airline's requirement; the market development and sales representatives must know from the start when an airline is considering new equipment. This is important from the sales pitch standpoint—each manufacturer wants to be the first to demonstrate what its equipment can do, sometimes offering to do specific route studies on how its airplanes would fit each airline's specific needs on its particular routes. Projections on how advances in future equipment technologies might benefit the customer, as well as financing prospects and how financing can be arranged, need to be introduced into the sales equation at an early stage.

tain close contact with the airlines at the middle and upper management level. They also track the pulse of an airline's fleet requirements while continually feeding the manufacturer's current thinking on equipment, modifications, and new types under development.

Bringing potential customers into the factory is another important part of the sale—much like a car dealer getting a prospect into the show room. Although airliners do not have "sticker prices," Douglas's products sell within these ranges: MD-90s $35–$40 million; MD-80s $30 million; MD-11s $100 million plus; and the new MD-95s $20–$25 million. Each aircraft manufacturer will have customers and potential customers visiting the factory literally on a daily basis. Douglas is currently showing off its full-scale MD-95 mock-up and, once that has been seen, customers are taken to the "product display area." This is a large

area filled with full-scale mock-ups of the company's aircraft, their cockpits and cabins, and also models of engines. The product display area is Douglas's version of the automobile showroom. Also, if it's timely, sales representatives will take potential customers through one of the airplanes on the production line to see the quality and craftsmanship built into each aircraft.

When Douglas makes a new aircraft delivery, the product display area is used for news briefings or large gatherings. It is surrounded by conference and meeting rooms. Part of the continuing dialog with the airlines is frequent meetings where the manufacturer assembles as many airline repre-

A coveted MD-90 logo sticker for application on well-traveled crew briefcases only. *McDonnell Douglas*

The MD-90 is the "third generation" of the DC-9, the prototype of which is shown in flight over Southern California. The DC-9 made its first flight on February 25, 1965. The company has sold 976 DC-9s and 1,108 "second generation" MD-80-series aircraft. *McDonnell Douglas*

For the MD-90 design, Douglas engineers refined the proven cockpit of the MD-80. Because of the similarities between the two cockpits, transition training to the MD-90 is minimal. This fact will save airlines thousands of dollars per pilot in training costs. *McDonnell Douglas*

Powered by twin International Aero Engines (IAE) V2500 engines, the first test-flight aircraft (T-1) is seen during its test-flight program. *McDonnell Douglas*

Usually, after due deliberation and having listened to sales pitches from the three major airliner manufacturers (Boeing, Douglas, and Airbus), the customer airline will issue a formal request for proposals. They will send the same request (specifications) to all competing manufacturers. That's when the game gets hot. This is where the competition in airplane capability, economics of operation, and financing gets serious. The request for proposal will usually spell out in detail specifications for interiors, engine capabilities, and other unique requirements.

Once an airline receives all of the proposals, they are given an exhaustive technical and economic evaluation to determine which aircraft type the airline wants to purchase. After the purchase decision has been made, the customer airline and manufacturer enter configuration discussions. Each airline has its own ideas on some elements of the configuration of the airplane. In these discussions, technical representatives from the airline and the manufacturer hammer out the finer minutia, such as avionics choices (e.g., whether it will be a Honeywell compass or an Allied Signal compass).

Working Together to Ensure a Quality Product

Ronald W. Allen, chairman, president, and chief executive officer of Delta Air Lines, said, "The MD-90 is an aircraft designed for Delta's future. From the start, we participated in writing the specifications for this aircraft in anticipation of where our industry and our company are headed." The airline assembled teams of its employees to funnel information and design suggestions to the manufacturer beginning in 1989. Seeing the results of the two companies' combined five-year effort, Delta placed a firm order for 31 aircraft with options for an additional aircraft, becoming the MD-90's launch customer.

Ship T-1 made its first flight on February 22, 1993, beginning a thorough test-flight program.
McDonnell Douglas

Douglas's plan for the MD-90 was to re-engine the MD-88 so that it would be capable of meeting anticipated Stage 4 noise reduction levels, reduce the interior cabin noise, increase fuel efficiency, and cut down on the level of exhaust emissions. Douglas sought to do all this while maintaining the same pilot type rating as for the MD-80 series, and addressing the items that caused the most in-service delays.

When the two companies met, Delta presented Douglas with a list of 10 problem areas affecting dispatch reliability. If Douglas could address these problems, they would have one of the most reliable airliners in the world. The most recurring items included, with delays per 1,000 departures in parenthe-

ses: alternating current generation and control (0.45); the auxiliary power unit (0.37); nose landing gear (0.30); Digital Flight Guidance Computer (0.28); Landing Gear Position Indicator (0.27); main-landing-gear wheels and tires (0.26); stall warning system (0.25); compass system (0.25); main brake control (0.24); and the engine fuel control (0.24).

During the early design development stages of a new model, airline employees come to the manufacturer to give their input and guidance. This is typically done in two or three different groups—a cockpit group, a cabin- and passenger-service group, and a maintenance and support group. Once Delta's concerns and requirements were discussed, Douglas engineers quickly

addressed those items. First, the electrical system was replaced with a modular Variable-Speed, Constant-Frequency (VSCF) system that will prevent power surges and extend the service lives of other electrical components. Douglas selected the Allied Signal/Garrett 131-9(D) auxiliary power unit (APU) to meet the increased needs of the aircraft's upgraded systems and new engines. New software was written for the Digital Flight Guidance Computer, and the stall warning system was upgraded. The compass system's problems were eliminated by the installation of an Inertial Reference System (IRS), and a new engine electronic controller solved the fuel control problem. The remaining squawks were associated with the land-

The MD-90-30 seats 153-passengers, and production is expected to last well into the next century. *McDonnell Douglas*

ing gear. New 21-inch wheels and tires were added, as was a new spray deflector for the nose wheel. The brakes were replaced with carbon units reducing total aircraft weight by 400 pounds. Also incorporated was an independent dual-brake-valve system featuring digital antiskid controls, a brake temperature monitoring system, and in-flight ram-air cooling. The landing gear position indicator had a new modified lens-cap assembly installed.

Once Delta's main concerns had been addressed by the Douglas designers, they began refining the MD-90's cockpit to incorporate 1990s technologies. Considered as a "third-generation DC-9," the new MD-90s are similar enough to the MD-88 that they offer Delta a tremendous savings in pilot transition and recurrency training costs. For pilots, the flight deck layout is familiar: the MD-90 retains the MD-88 Electronic Flight Instrument System (EFIS). Improvements made to existing equipment include an improved Flight Management System (FMS) and solid-state engine and systems displays, new software to drive the wind-shear computer, a solid-state overhead annunciator panel, and ARINC 700 series

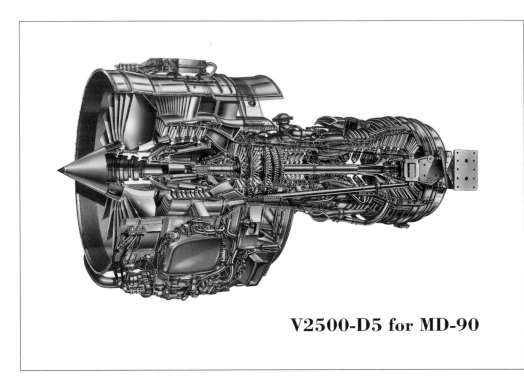

V2500-D5 for MD-90

Cut-away of the V2500-D5 that powers the MD-90-series twin-jets. *McDonnell Douglas*

RIGHT: The first production MD-90 lifts off from Long Beach on its maiden flight, September 20, 1994. Its first flight lasted 3 hours and 30 minutes. *McDonnell Douglas*

avionics upgrades. New equipment in the cockpit includes an auxiliary control system, a Master Caution and Warning computer, an Air Data computer, and the IRS. These improvements increase cockpit systems reliability and reduce maintenance while minimizing possible errors and crew member workload.

Structurally, the MD-90 maintains the MD-83 fuselage, with the addition of a 57-inch plug forward of the wings. The MD-90 incorporates a strengthened MD-83 wing, and the tail and horizontal group are from the MD-87. This installation also features a powered elevator and rudder capable of reverting to manual control. The ailerons remain unboosted and trim-tab flown. The MD-90's overall length is 152 feet, 7 inches and its wing span is 107 feet, 10 inches. The plane cruises at Mach 0.76 or roughly 500 miles per hour and has a maximum gross takeoff weight of 156,000 pounds.

A new vacuum lavatory system was also installed on the MD-90. This system offers single-point servicing, reducing aircraft turnaround time and possible airframe corrosion. To save weight and increase the reliability of certain components, composites were used in 25 different structural areas, from the rudders, ailerons, and trim tabs to the wing-fillet fairings, tail cone, and cargo-compartment floors and liners.

To cut manufacturing costs and streamline the assembly process, Douglas has instituted a modular assembly concept for the MD-90. This allows the company to use its shop floor space more efficiently. Subassemblies of major fuselage sections can be accomplished off-site where, for instance, the fuselage panels and other subassemblies will be collected from subcontractors. Here, these small parts will come

Delta touts the MD-90 as "Our Aircraft for the Future." N902DA (msn 53382) was one of the first three MD-90s to join Delta's fleet. *McDonnell Douglas*

Airframe Configuration
MD-90

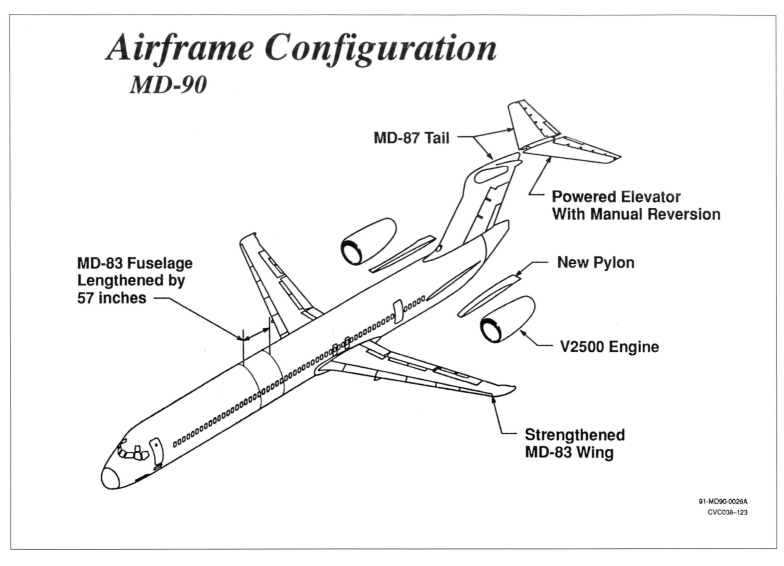

MD-87 Tail

Powered Elevator
With Manual Reversion

MD-83 Fuselage
Lengthened by
57 inches

New Pylon

V2500 Engine

Strengthened
MD-83 Wing

91-MD90-0026A
CVC038–123

The airframe configuration chart distinctly shows where the "third-generation DC-9" gets its parts from. The tail, rudder, horizontal, and elevators come directly from the MD-87. These MD-87 parts are coupled to an improved and strengthened MD-83 wing and lengthened MD-83 fuselage. New engines and redesigned pylons complete the exterior make-over. *McDonnell Douglas*

together to form a module such as the nose section or forward fuselage. These modules are then shipped to Long Beach, California, for final assembly, where they are attached to other sections to form a complete aircraft. This modular-assembly concept also allows Douglas to build both the MD-80 series and MD-90 aircraft on the same assembly line.

Aircraft longevity was another concern. Technology has greatly improved since the early 1960s when the DC-9 was designed for a life span of 30,000 flying hours or 40,000 landings.

The MD-83 has a Design Service Life Goal (DSLG) of 50,000 hours and landings, while the MD-90's DSLG is planned for 90,000 hours and 60,000 landings. Of course, if an airline wants to invest the capital into an aircraft service life extension program, an airliner can fly indefinitely, or until it is uneconomical—either in maintenance or fuel-consumption costs. Although this number is constantly changing, the high-time DC-9 (Fuselage 21) had recently logged 95,396 hours, more than three times its expected life span.

Clean Burning, Fuel Efficient V2525-D5 Engines

Now that Douglas had obtained input from the airline operators, the second key to the MD-90's success came with the selection of the International Aero Engines (IAE) V2525-D5 engine. (IAE is a consortium of Pratt & Whitney [US], Rolls Royce [U.K.], Fiat Avio [Italy], MTU [Germany], and JAEC [Japan].) Once this engine was mated to the proposed MD-90, Douglas knew they had a product that was ready for the 21st century.

The first MD-90 for JAS, JA8062 (msn 53352), is elevated off the assembly-line floor for easy movement down the line. *Nicholas A. Veronico/*Airliners *Magazine*

The IAE V2500 series of power-plants are all identical internally. The only difference between the MD-90's V2525-D5 and the Airbus A320's V2500-A1 is the exterior mounting and the Douglas-modified nacelle. Both engines have been rated as producing 25,000 pounds of thrust each, excellent for high density-altitude operations.

The V2525-D5 also features a cockpit-selectable 3,000-pound-thrust boost for operations from hot, high airports. In the past, an engine and the software that controls it were certified to a single thrust level. If an operator planned to fly the engine at higher thrust settings than certified, the engine manufacturers would "increase the price of the engine for that added thrust because it degrades the reliability and adds to the spares need and puts more stress and strain on the engine," said Grace M. Robertson, vice president and general manager of the MD-90 twin-jet program. "So, consequently, the cost of the engine goes up. In this case, you can select it [3,000 pounds of added boost] and use it only when you need it, and the engine manufacturer can have confidence that you are not going to run with that thrust unless you need it. That helps reduce the price of the engine for the operators, improves the reliability, and gives them the capability if needed. Very few operators need hot, high performance on every takeoff. It's a flexibility that should have a lot of value."

Douglas is only offering the V2525-D5 engine for the MD-90. Robertson said that the "decision to only offer one engine type was made with an absolutely firm conviction that this was the best engine and that there wasn't anything near it. We are willing to take the risk of being exclusive on this decision because there really wasn't a competitive engine as good. I believe that more every day."

Another Delta MD-90 nears completion at Long Beach. Both the MD-80 and MD-90 series are built in this quarter-mile-long building. *Nicholas A. Veronico/*Airliners *Magazine*

A close-up of the MD-90's new engine pylon. Note the thickness and the aerodynamic properties of the pylon. *Nicholas A. Veronico/*Airliners *Magazine*

The V2500 series is reportedly 10 percent more efficient than other engines in its thrust class. At current jet fuel prices, Delta projects that they will save $200,000 per year per aircraft when compared to the fuel costs of an MD-88. Robert Rosati, IAE president, said, "Experience has shown that the V2500 will save Delta money in operating costs, while providing the reliable, on-time performance Delta passengers

The MD-90 gets its horizontal and vertical sections from the MD-87. Aircraft N87MD (msn 49388) made its first flight on December 4, 1986, and has been retained by Douglas for test work. *Nicholas A. Veronico/Airliners Magazine*

expect. It's a rugged, dependable engine that incorporates the best technology from around the world."

Recently, many European countries have begun regulating engine exhaust emissions. The V2500 series reportedly produces less than one-fifth of the pollutants allowed by those regulations.

When full takeoff power is applied, the MD-90 is quieter than any airliner in its class. "The MD-90 demonstrates Delta's commitment to comply with or exceed government noise regulations," Delta CEO Allen said. "In fact, the MD-90 operates more quietly than regulations will require in the year 2000."

Why is the MD-90 the quietest twin-jet? The solution to reducing the MD-80 series' noise signature began with the new engine. It was designed to be quieter than previous engines, and its noise footprint was further reduced by the MD-90s rear fuselage mounting. When coupled with an airport-neighbor-friendly flight profile, the wing shields those on the ground from the noise as the plane approaches. Daryl N. May, Ph.D., group leader for acoustics from Douglas's Aerodynamics and Acoustics Design and Technology group, said, "When we wanted to improve on the MD-80, clearly noise was one of the most important

improvements we could bring to it. The new engine brings improved economy and it may well bring improved reliability, but it also had to bring improved acoustical properties.

"The first design principle brought to the engine for quiet noise properties is that it is a high-bypass engine—meaning that the airflow rates out of the exhaust are much lower than they are with predecessor engines. Thus the jet noise of the overall component is reduced. There are other acoustical features such as the long duct nacelle, which favors acoustics and aerodynamics in this configuration. The long duct

This DC-9-82 (MD-82), I-DATJ (msn 53227), is seen on the Long Beach final assembly ramp, January 14, 1995. The plane was test flown, completely painted, and accepted by the customer, Alitalia, 12 days later, on January 26. *Nicholas A. Veronico/Airliners Magazine*

nacelle has extensive acoustical treatment in it, and we brought to the V2500 some extra treatment to the tail cone by virtue of a hot stream exhaust liner.

"Then there are a number of features we put into the airplane partly in the engine and partly beyond the engine for cabin noise reduction. We have been successful in reducing the cabin noise five or six decibels in the back with a weight reduction [compared with the MD-80] of 64 pounds."

Installation of the V2500 on the MD-90 called for a new engine pylon to be designed. According to May, "The engine pylons are quite substantial for aerodynamic reasons. They are a thicker

pylon and have a significant structural benefit in that they are deeper and able to carry the load with less pylon weight. There was also an acoustical benefit in that the increased structure could attenuate the noise between the engine and the fuselage."

Benefits for the Passenger

The traveling public will enjoy the MD-90's large seats, aisle, and generous overhead baggage capacity—12 percent per passenger larger than on other narrow-bodies. The overhead also features a fully lighted handrail grip that runs the length of the interior. After takeoff, the lower interior noise levels—a

direct result of the quieter engine, engine placement and mounting, and new sound proofing—will increase cabin comfort and reduce traveler fatigue. For noise comparison purposes, with the exception of the last 10 seating rows, the interior noise level of the MD-90 is said to equal that of the A320's first-class section.

The MD-90 can accommodate three different seating configurations. The standard mixed-class interior features 12 first class seats with a 36-inch pitch and 141 economy seats ranging in pitch from a narrow 31 inches to 33 inches. For the operator with single-class service in mind, the MD-90 can be configured to seat 163 or 172 passengers,

Each V2500 engine produces 25,000 pounds of thrust. Large cowl panels provide easy access for inspections of the powerplants. *Nicholas A. Veronico/*Airliners *Magazine*

Aerodynamic properties of the engine pylon can be seen in this rear view. *Nicholas A. Veronico/*Airliners *Magazine*

depending on seat pitch (29 inches being the tightest). Delta will introduce the MD-90 with a 153-seat, five-abreast interior.

Factory Flight Testing, Training, and of course, Paperwork

The first delivery of a new airliner type to an airline calls for a celebration. Customer airline executives and those of the manufacturer join journalists, community leaders, and local, city, state, and federal representatives in delivering the new jetliner. On subsequent deliveries, the airline only sends its acceptance crew. There are no parties, brass bands, or VIPs. They just pick up the keys, sign the papers, and fly the new airliner home.

Once an airplane is completely assembled, it is rolled into the paint hangar. When a plane is put into the paint shop, it takes four or five days to mask, paint, and detail. Sometimes due to schedule, or if other aircraft need to be painted at the same time, aircraft are flown to an outside facility, but this is a rare exception.

From paint, a new aircraft will be rolled to the flight ramp where it is prepared with fuel system checks and a final review of all onboard systems. Then the plane is fueled and the engines are run and tuned.

The maiden flight has members of Douglas's production test-flight crew at the controls. They take it up for a 4- or 5-hour flight to wring out every system in the airplane. Upon landing, if there are things that need to be fixed, they are corrected. Then production test pilots fly it again to verify that all items have been fixed and are functioning properly. Shortly thereafter, the airline acceptance pilots arrive and make their own test flight of the airplane. Once again, all of the systems are thoroughly wrung out. If no problems arise on the first flight, they sign it off. If the acceptance pilots find items that they want adjusted, the items are repaired, and then the plane is flown again. It is almost an industry standard that the manufacturer's pilots will fly the plane no more than twice, and the airline's acceptance crews will only need one test flight before signing for the airliner.

Douglas test flight employs between 50 and 60 pilots, with about 200 people in the department. In addition to testing the new planes before delivery to the airlines, this department's work-load includes developing flight operations manuals for each Douglas model and its derivatives, working with the airline cus-

Aircraft N275WA (msn 48631), an MD-11CF (Convertible Freighter, with interchangeable interior for passengers or freight), was originally delivered to World Airways who subsequently leased it to Garuda Indonesian Airways. After that carrier returned the wide-body, it was then configured as a full-freighter and sub-leased to Malaysia Airlines in July 1995. *Nicholas A. Veronico/Airliners Magazine*

N979VJ (msn 47372), a DC-9-31, was first delivered to Allegheny Airlines and is seen here after the company merged to become USAir. In October 1995, the plane was withdrawn from service and stored at Evergreen Air Center, Marana, Arizona. *George Hall/Check Six*

Delta MD-11 N801DE over the blue waters of the Pacific Ocean prior to delivery. *George Hall/Check Six*

N801DE (msn 48472) was the first of its type to fly for Delta Air Lines. The carrier took delivery of the tri-jet on March 13, 1992. *George Hall/Check Six*

tomer to add in acceptable revisions that fit a particular airline's operating preferences, and then obtaining Federal Aviation Administration (FAA) approval. Factory pilots also maintain a dialog with airline flight operations departments monitoring "how goes it" with Douglas products. This often involves factory pilots getting in and flying the line with customer airlines. Using what they learn on the line allows the Douglas pilots to return to the factory and develop procedures that can be more effective and efficient, or to take care of problems. They also use their line flying as an opportunity to share techniques learned from the pilots of other airlines.

The manufacturer's test-flight department also serves as the first flight-crew trainers for any airplane. Typically, they will train an airline's instructor crews (depending on the size of the airline). If it is a smaller airline, the manufacturer may train all of its crews. Flight-crew training is a very important part of an airline manufacturer's business.

Training is also a valuable way of bringing airline personnel to the fac-

tory. When they come in for flight training, crews will usually stay anywhere from one to four weeks—an excellent opportunity to put the manufacturer's best people and products on display.

Like a new car, a jetliner does come with a warranty—typically three-years on the structure and parts. That's where it gets tricky for the manufacturer. Although Douglas delivers the warranty to the customer airline, all of the component and systems suppliers must hold up their end of the bargain by honoring their warranties to both the airplane manufacturer and the customer airline.

When the first aircraft of a type is delivered, the manufacturer will have been working with that airline for a period of months developing the flight-crew training and operations manuals, the maintenance manuals, and completing all of the technical documentation to

An aerial view of the Douglas final assembly ramp, December 1978. Here aircraft are prepared for their maiden flight. *George Hall/Check Six*

The prototype MD-11 (msn 48401) made its first flight on January 10, 1990. It was retained by McDonnell Douglas for testing and FAA certification and was then sold to FedEx. *George Hall/Check Six*

support the airplane. All of the manuals must meet FAA approval before an aircraft can begin flying passengers.

Often, after an airline takes delivery of a new type, they may use the plane for training before beginning service. Typically, when an airline receives a new type, Federal Aviation Regulations (FARs) require they perform "proving runs" before they inaugurate revenue service. Proving runs require an airline to operate the new type to the stations it will be serving in revenue service. This is done just to show that everything is going to work the way it is supposed to work—the ground handling equipment is compatible with the new plane, it can be catered in the allot-ted time, baggage can be loaded and unloaded efficiently, and so on.

First Flights, Certification, and Delivery

The prototype MD-90 flew for the first time on February 22, 1993. "The huge performance gain is really seen during the takeoff," said Douglas test pilot G. R. "Bear" Smith. Chief Test Pilot William Jones, Smith flying as copilot, and flight engineer Barry McCarthy crewed the MD-90's first flight. "Your climb rate from sea level to 10 or 15,000 feet is absolutely awesome," continued Smith. "It's amazing. You are climbing at 5, 6, 7,000 feet per minute with a 140–150,000 pound plane. That performance shows itself when you get to an airport that's got high altitude and you've got heavy weight and need a little extra thrust. You select the 28,000-pound-thrust rating and down the road you go. That's what the big engines are for. It's not to go faster at altitude, it's to get the weight airborne."

For an MD-88 flight officer to transition into the MD-90 requires that the pilot attend a three- to six-day differences class and two two-hour simulator sessions to get the feel of new overhead and instrument panels and switch locations. That's all. A tremendous amount of work went into achieving this type commonality and eliminating any confusion factor between the MD-88 and MD-90.

Registered N601FE and named *Christy*, the freighter joined FedEx's fleet on June 27, 1991. *George Hall/Check Six*

The first production model, wearing Delta colors, took to the skies on September 20, 1994. Shortly after that flight, Grace M. Robertson joined the Douglas team as vice president and general manager of the MD-90 twin-jet program. Prior to taking the reins at the MD-90 program, Robertson had been employed by Boeing for the past 17 years, most recently as director of 747 and 767 derivatives.

The MD-90 was certified by the FAA on November 16, 1994. Bob Hood, president of Douglas Aircraft Company, accepted the type and production certificates from Transportation Secretary Frederico Pena during ceremonies held in Washington, D.C. The FAA worked closely with Douglas to accomplish the joint type and production certification.

Upon certification, the MD-90 had flown 1,900 hours and met or exceeded all technical objectives set by the company. The MD-90's fly-over noise was quieter than predicted; the plane exceeded the cruise performance guarantees; was certified for CAT IIIa Autoland, and the FMS also met with FAA approval; the FAA granted that the MD-80-series type rating would be extended to the MD-90; and the interior noise was lowest in the plane's class. High standards set, high standards met.

When the MD-90 was certified, Douglas reported that they had invested almost $250 million over five years on the plane's development as well as 3 million man-hours.

"The program focus is now on a successful delivery, meeting all of our commitments to our customers," said Robertson. "We believe that there is nothing we can do in marketing the airplane that is as important as having Delta say 'that McDonnell Douglas delivered on schedule and they delivered the product as promised, they are supporting the product, they are being responsive to our entry into service needs.' We have the opportunity for the next six months to be right there with Delta, not only helping them incorporate the airplane into their systems, but to solve any problems that inevitably

N946AS (msn 49658), a DC-9 83 (MD-83), is operated by Alaska Airlines of Seattle, Washington, and was delivered to the carrier in February 1990. *Rafe Tomsett/Check Six*

N601FE touches down as a Delta 767 and Morris Air 737 await permission to depart. *George Hall/Check Six*

show up. We will be able to focus and to really be responsive to Delta's needs."

Delta began scheduled service with the MD-90 on April 1, 1995. The type operates from the company's Dallas/Ft. Worth hub to cities in the Midwest and on the Eastern Seaboard. The airline currently has a fleet of 544 aircraft that serve 211 cities spanning 32 countries throughout the world.

Branching Out After the Launch Customer Takes Delivery

The MD-90 program has delivered 33 aircraft to date, and has 112 firm orders with 72 options and reservations from Delta Air Lines, Japan Air System (JAS), Great China Airlines, EVA Air of Taiwan, Hwa-Hsia Corporation also of Taiwan, Kibris Turk Hava Yolari (KTHY) of Turkey, GATX Capital Corporation, and the China National Aero-Technology Import/Export Corporation (CATIC). Through a trunk-liner agreement, amended November 4, 1994, 20 MD-90s will be built in China. Those aircraft, and 20 MD-80-series planes also ordered, make the deal with China worth $1.6 billion to Douglas. The 20 MD-90s are included in the firm orders number.

Tail section and number two engine nacelle are mated to form the beginnings of a new MD-11. *Sam Sargent/Check Six*

MD-80 series jetliners progress down the Long Beach assembly line. *Sam Sargent/Check Six*

During a stock-photo shoot for a future Alaska Airlines advertisement, airliner and photo plane cruise over San Francisco, California. *Rafe Tomsett/Check Six*

By retracting the flaps, landing gear, spoilers, and slats, the flightcrew can configure the Delta MD-11 for economic cruising at 473 knots. Fuel efficiency is paramount for airlines to keep their costs down and airfares inexpensive. *George Hall/Check Six*

Is Douglas looking to the future of its twin-jet program after the successful introduction of the MD-90? Yes. The company has plans for an extended-range version, the MD-90-30ER; a high-density-seating version, the MD-90-35; and a brawnier version, the MD-90-50 featuring strengthened wing, fuselage, and horizontal and vertical stabilizers and powered by 28,000-pound V2528-D5 engines for an increased maximum gross takeoff weight. Also in the works is a high-density MD-90-55. Another new product nearing introduction is the 100-seat MD-95. The plane will be powered by BMW/Rolls-Royce engines and final assembly will take place at the proposed Douglas Delivery Center in Dallas, Texas, that will be supervised by Dalfort Aviation. The company met with possible MD-95 launch customers in Berlin, Germany, in November 1994 and at that time announced its international team of contractor-partners from the United States, Europe, Asia, and the Middle East. ValuJet Airlines of Atlanta, Georgia, at one time an operator of almost 50 DC-9-series aircraft, was the MD-95's launch customer placing an order for 50 in 1995. Douglas projects a worldwide sales demand of 1,700 MD-95s over the next 20 years.

Here the wingtip fuel tank of the Learjet photo ship is clearly visible below the nose of a FedEx MD-11. The 169 foot wingspan of the MD-11 is a constant concern whenever aircraft are flying in close formation. *George Hall/Check Six*

RIGHT: The MD-11F is the freighter version of the standard MD-11. FedEx fills its main and lower decks with pallets and containers loaded with packages. When fully loaded, the MD-11 can takeoff with a maximum weight of over 625,500 pounds. *George Hall/Check Six*

Delta Air Lines saves on crew costs by flying the MD-11. With its six screen electronic flight instrumentation system, the MD-11 can be flown with a flightcrew of two instead of the three required by the DC-10. *George Hall/Check Six*

A Delta Air Lines MD-11 returns home after a photo shoot out over the Pacific Ocean.
George Hall/Check Six

Port and starboard views of one of Continental Airlines' DC-10s. Continental can utilize the DC-10's impressive range of over 6,500 nautical miles, or trade range for extra payload and fly additional weight over shorter distances. The DC-10 has a maximum takeoff weight of 580,000 pounds. *George Hall/Check Six*

CHAPTER 2

A DAY IN THE LIFE OF A JETLINER

Before a single passenger arrives for the first flight of the day, the ground and flight crews are at the airport preparing the aircraft. Their support staff, the aircraft dispatchers, have spent hours reviewing data and preparing for the day ahead. Safety, on the ground and in the air, is the first priority of each and every airline employee. For many, their lives depend on it. Over the years, strict procedures have been developed for every airline operation.

Tom W. Birkley, a licensed aircraft dispatcher for American Trans Air (ATA), prepares for his workday by viewing the Weather Channel before he leaves home. He is concerned with

The first officer completes a walk-around inspection of the aircraft before the hydraulic system is initialized. After the system has been run through its checks, the aircraft is again visually inspected, ensuring that all hydraulically operated surfaces have closed properly and the system has not leaked. *George Hall/Check Six*

QANTAS jetliner VH-OGF, a Boeing 767-338 (ER, msn 24853), named *City of Lismore*, nears its destination, Sydney, Australia. *George Hall/Check Six*

After the crew briefing, the pilots head to their office, where they perform a series of checklists before the first passengers board. *Katsu Tokunaga/Check Six*

weather patterns both at home and abroad. Some days he works the international desk and others the domestic desk. Knowing the weather ahead of time prepares him for the challenges he, and other dispatchers around him, must meet.

As a licensed dispatcher, Birkley and the plane's pilot share equal responsibility for the safe operation of all phases of the flight. Testing for dispatchers is similar to testing for the Air Transport Pilot (ATP) rating, involving both a written and oral, or practical, test. Dispatchers also complete a ground-school class for each type of aircraft they will be working with. They are required to fly 5 hours per

year in the cockpit's jump seat, observing how the flight crew interacts.

ATA's dispatch office, located in Indianapolis, Indiana, employs 28 licensed dispatchers overseeing flights on the domestic and international desks. An "overflow" desk does just as the name implies, handling both international and domestic flights. American Trans Air runs between 150 and 200 flights per day and a usual shift at ATA would use four desks—a domestic, an international, an assistant supervisor, and the dispatch supervisor. A larger airline, such as United, employs a little more than 140 dispatchers who work

sections of the route system rather than domestic or international desks.

Upon arrival at his office, Birkley reads the company "hot board" displaying daily updates of Air Traffic Control (ATC) advisories. He then checks delays system-wide and flow control into certain cities such as San Francisco, Los Angeles, Chicago, and Boston. Severe weather limits the number of aircraft that can be landed simultaneously at these airports, so the flow of planes must be regulated.

After reviewing all pertinent information, he then takes over a desk from the previous shift's dispatcher,

An America West Airbus A320-231, N627AW (msn 066), awaits ground crews that will prepare it for the first flight of the day.

who might have 10–20 flights in progress. First, the pilot status reports are reviewed for each flight. Then, a quick check of the en route weather for each flight is made to see if a flight will have to be re-routed around a severe storm system. "I put a lot of faith in the previous dispatcher," Birkley said, "that he or she has done their job as far as the routing of a flight, that they've checked the weather en route, and reviewed all of the NOTAMs [NOtice To AirMen]." Dispatchers must trust those who ran

The ground crew positions belt loaders at the cargo hatches and then loads any freight and mail to be delivered to the aircraft's next destination. *Joe Towers/Check Six*

Smaller aircraft use airstairs for boarding rather than jetways. Here, passengers file out of the terminal past a waiting Air Cal BAe 146-200A, N145AC (msn E2055). This aircraft is now operated by Malmo Aviation of Malmo-Sturup, Sweden, and is registered SE-DRF. *George Hall/Check Six*

Once the aircraft has been boarded and the paperwork handed to the gate agent, the captain gives the lead flight attendant permission to close the cabin door. Here, the door has been closed on an American Eagle Saab 340B, and the cockpit crew is preparing to start the engines. Notice that the wing-tip navigation lights are on. N243AE (msn 243) was delivered to American Eagle on May 16, 1991. *Joe Towers/Check Six*

the prior shift because they don't have time to double-check all of the paperwork for the 20 or so flights for which they are assuming responsibility. Each is a highly trained, licensed professional. Once Birkley takes over, those 20 flights are then his, and if anything goes wrong, it is his responsibility.

Now in charge of his desk, Birkley reviews the flights he must plan. At ATA, each flight requiring a dispatcher's attention is provided on a single form. Again, he will chart the weather for all flights in his area of responsibility—both flights en route and those he will plan. Each flight plan is completed one at a time. First, an aircraft capable of flying the route with the scheduled number of passengers is selected and assigned by tail number (registration). Any open or deferred maintenance items are reviewed to ensure that aircraft can legally and safely fly according to the FARs. Next, the aircraft model is reviewed. "One of the interesting things I run into now is with the Boeing 727," said Birkley. "I think we have nine different models with eight different engine types with three or four different navigation systems and two or three different fuel system setups. You can get yourself in a bind if you don't pay attention to the particular aircraft you are assigning to a selected route.

"I look at the status sheet to see if the aircraft in question has auxiliary tanks, and what type navigation system (for example, Global Positioning System [GPS] or VLF-Omega [very low frequency]) it has. All of our aircraft use JT-8D engines on the 727s, but it could be JT-8D-9, -15, -15A, -17, -17A, -17R, and each engine type's capability determines climb-out performance and maximum gross takeoff weight. For some of the marginal airports we fly out of, any field with runways under 7,000 feet, such as Chicago-Midway, if we don't have -15, or -17 engines the flight will be weight restricted."

Lufthansa McDonnell Douglas DC-10 D-ADKO (msn 47929), named *Stuttgart*, prepares to take on fuel. Lufthansa phased out its DC-10 fleet in the early 1990s, and 47929 now flies with Skyjet Brazil, re-registered PP-AJM. *Joe Towers/Check Six*

Next, Birkley reviews the departure airport. He is concerned with wind direction and what the forecast winds are for departure time. This will determine the runway to be used for takeoff, which in turn dictates the payload, or number of passengers. For shorter routes, flights are restricted by the landing weight the destination airport's runways can safely handle. Takeoff weight is more of a factor on longer routes; how much weight the aircraft can lift at departure is the determining factor.

The route of flight is then reviewed. Some airlines use a fixed route each trip, but the route might be modified on a given day to save fuel or avoid bad weather. "What I use here at ATA is a system called 'Dynamic Flight

Planning' where the computer selects the path of least resistance," said Birkley. "We take advantage of the winds aloft that day. We try to do this on most of our longer flights. It can make a 10- or 15-minute difference versus using the same route every day. This adds up to a significant savings, so we are constantly monitoring these options. We must also make sure the airplane scheduled for the route has the navigation systems compatible with this type of flying." When considering a particular route, turbulence and any pilot reports (PiReps) of turbulence encountered are also reviewed. Mother Nature can throw curves at the dispatchers in other ways, so the dispatchers must route flights

around hurricanes and tropical storms. Active volcanos are also a consideration; in fact, according to Birkley, "these must be avoided at all costs" because catastrophic engine failure can result from ingestion of volcanic ash.

When working the international desk, overflight permissions must be obtained from each country along the flight's intended path. It can take up to one week to receive overflight permission from some countries. If the permission has not been received, a flight must be flown outside a nation's borders—an expensive proposition. "Sometimes a country will provide us with an overflight number, and then as the flight is about to cross their border, their air traf-

American Airlines Boeing 767-323 (ER [extended range]) N361AA (msn 24042) is pushed back from the gate prior to engine start. *Joe Towers/Check Six*

fic controllers will say that the number is incorrect, refusing permission to enter their airspace," said Birkley. "We are then forced to fly around their borders, and sometimes we will not have enough fuel for that. This forces us to divert and land for fuel somewhere. This causes lengthy delays at the destination airport. We try to pre-plan and avoid potential problems," continued Birkley. "I will file an international flight plan 4–6 hours in advance, listing all of the over-flight permission numbers. This is sent to each country along the route; that way if there is any problem or question it can be resolved as soon as possible. It can go as far as contacting an embassy to help get overflight permission." Certain countries in the Middle and Far East area are extremely "touchy," while the majority of European countries are "flight plan only."

After a route has been selected, the destination airport's runway config-uration is reviewed. Considerations include which runway will be used for landing, if the flight will be light enough to use this particular runway, and whether the plane can safely stop in the distance available if the brake's antiskid control becomes inoperative. Then, an alternate airport is selected in case the flight must be diverted due to bad weather or runway closure, and the same landing criteria are reviewed for the alternate airport.

Birkley then factors in whether or not to load additional fuel. It costs fuel to carry fuel, but Birkley said, "I'm not shy about doing it if the destination airport is marginal." Worldwide fuel prices are provided to the dispatchers by ATA's fuel department. These figures give dispatchers the option of carrying extra fuel, or "tankering." This is done when fuel prices at the destination airport are 20–50 cents per gallon higher than at the originating airport. Even if a small amount of fuel is added at the destination airport, tankering can save thousands of dollars per trip, but the costs must be weighed against the penalty of the heavily loaded aircraft's performance.

All of the variables mentioned are entered into the flight release, which consists of a copy of the flight plan; all pertinent weather information for the flight's origin, destination, and alternate airports and any PiReps for the en route portion of the trip; and all NOTAMs that could affect the flight or any airports along its route. This information, collectively known as a "flight plan," is sent from the dispatch office to the flight's origin station by computer. Regulations also require the dispatcher to provide the latest weather at time of departure. This information is often faxed to the plane at the terminal gate. The dispatcher then files the flight plan by computerwith air traffic control.

At the Airport

While the dispatcher is planning a flight, dozens of others are working feverishly to prepare the plane and its passengers for the trip.

When the ground crew arrives, they first position belt loaders near the belly cargo hatches in preparation for loading. Mail and freight is then loaded according to destination city.

One hour before departure, the flight crew —pilot, copilot, and flight engineer (although most aircraft now fly without a flight engineer)—will meet.

A view past the Continental gates with a pair of McDonnell Douglas DC-10s framed by two Boeing 747 tails. *Joe Towers/Check Six*

Turning onto the runway prior to takeoff is Delta Boeing 757 N624DL (msn 22914). This aircraft was delivered to the carrier on January 23, 1987. *Joe Towers/Check Six*

Once a positive rate of climb has been established, the gear is retracted. This takeoff photograph was arranged by the airline for George Hall's cameras at Mojave, California. *George Hall/Check Six*

The pilot will conduct the first meeting, reviewing time en route, weather (including turbulence reported by other flights), safety, security, and any other important procedures and aspects of what the day will entail.

After the cockpit crew adjourns to the aircraft, the flight attendants hold a briefing. For a coast-to-coast flight, on a DC-10 for example, there may be 12 flight attendants. During the briefing, the lead flight attendant assigns positions by seniority and qualifications. This determines which seat rows each attendant will be responsible for. Where a flight attendant sits determines his or her areas of responsibility, such as which exit he or she will be in charge of and what tasks he or she must accomplish during an emergency including use of oxygen, fire extinguishers, door slides, life vests, and rafts. Security of the aircraft on the ground and in the air is again reviewed.

Once on board, the flight attendants must complete a "pre-flight" checklist. First, each checks that his or her folding- or jump-seat is in working order and that all safety belts are functional. All switches and controls on the flight-attendant panel are checked for operation and proper settings. Then, each attendant inspects the exit door or doors, and the seating in his or her area of responsibility for safety concerns and to ensure that all life vests are properly stowed, overhead bins are clear, doors are latched properly, and so on.

Up Front

Arriving at the aircraft ahead of the flight attendants, the cockpit crew looks to see that no maintenance action is in process, where mechanics might have a flag over, for example, a hydraulic pump or an APU. The log book is read to see if the airplane's electrical system can be turned on without any problems—ensuring that maintenance is not in the middle of performing a service. The first flight crew of the day is greeted with a "cold airplane"—everything is off.

The captain enters the cockpit and checks the safety equipment—making sure life vests, crash ax, and required

After receiving clearance for takeoff, the pilots accelerate the aircraft, rotating at about 120 knots. Northwest Airlines 757 N517US (msn 23205), named *City of Portland*, seen here lifting off, is capable of carrying 14 first-class and 170 economy-class passengers. *George Hall/Check Six*

One pilot flies while the other operates the radios. Here, the captain has control of the aircraft, an MD-80. *Joe Towers/Check Six*

manuals are in place. External power is plugged in or the onboard APU is started. Once the electrical system is up and running, the cabin climate control system is set and turned on. The captain sits down, and at this point the first officer goes out and performs the walk-around inspection for the first flight of the day. After the inspection, the first officer indicates to the captain that all is clear to pressurize the hydraulic system. Then, the hydraulic checks of the flight controls are run through to ensure that the controls are doing what they are supposed to do. The system is then shut down, and the first officer walks around again, checking for any leaks or other problems such as a spoiler panel that has not retracted.

While the walk-around is being performed, the captain is completing the pre-flight check, which runs through all of the systems. This is done in a flow, starting at the very back of the upper panel and working on down. On the DC-9/MD-80 series, the essential circuit-breaker busses are located on the overhead panel. All of the others are situated behind the captain's seat. The most important are placed overhead so the crew has easy access and can very quickly detect if a breaker has tripped.

Working on down through the electrical system, the captain checks the five essential busses of the emergency power that control all of the gauges and various safety-of-flight items—everything

else is fail-safe, backed up by a manual, direct-cable backup. For example, if hydraulic control was lost to the elevators, there is a redundant cable system connected to the pilot's control yoke. During this pre-flight, the captain is looking for indications that an item is not working properly. If something is not working, maintenance is called immediately.

Still on the overhead panel, the captain finishes the electrical-system review, then checks the fuel system and its pumps. The flight-data recorders and cockpit-voice recorders (CVR) are tested to see that the indicator lights show they are operating properly. Various aircraft have different types of recorders. The DC-9/MD-80-series CVR will not work

Sunset at 39,000 feet, heading 246 degrees. An impressive view of the flight deck and sunset from a Boeing 757. *Joe Towers/Check Six*

with the engines off and the parking brake set. To check, the switch is turned to see that the "CVR off" lamp works properly. Some aircraft have tape-quality indicators—low, or "no good." As long as the pilot does not hear an audible warning indicating the tape is bad, the switch is turned back to the normal, guarded position. From here, the pilot works down through air conditioning and pressurization systems.

From the overhead, the flow moves to the digital flight guidance panel. Here the auto-land system is

The captain lines his Airbus A300 up on final to the runway, seen directly ahead of the windscreen centerbar. *Joe Towers/Check Six*

One of the most photographed landmarks in the United States also makes a great back-drop for an airline commercial. Here a Continental 747 passes over San Francisco's Golden Gate Bridge. *George Hall/Check Six*

tested. "That runs through a 55-second self test," said Captain Edward B. Cook of Reno Air. "When that is done you are looking to see that you don't have a 'No Auto Land' light. Then, switch it over to Number 2 and test the other side. Then, you set it up for the first part of the departure—the first couple of radial fixes that you need, altitudes and headings."

Working down to the captain's instruments, the pilot checks to see that the primary flight instruments are in agreement with the first officer's and with the standby attitude indicator. Next, the weather radar and its displays are reviewed. Some aircraft have the VLF-Omega system for area navigation. Pilots ensure that it is set up properly to navigate the flight legs of the day. Stored waypoints have been pre-loaded into the unit. If a pilot has to manually input the day's flight, he or she scrolls to the particular page where the waypoints are

entered and types in the identifier. If the waypoint has been stored in the system's memory base, the system will accept the identifier; if the waypoint has not been entered into the system, the pilot has to enter the latitude and longitude for the waypoint.

Next, the FMS's (Flight Management System's) computer is checked. Here, the settings are entered that will run the auto-throttles for the fuel-efficient optimum flight. The FMS moni-

Reno Air McDonnell Douglas DC-9-82 (MD-82, msn 49424) on short final approach. This aircraft is configured to seat 12 in first-class and 120 in economy-class seating. *Ted Carlson/Check Six*

Over the fence. Japan Airlines Boeing 777-246 JA8981 (msn 27364) is seen moments before touching down at Moses Lake, Washington. This aircraft first flew on January 26, 1996, and was delivered to the carrier on February 15, 1996. *George Hall/Check Six*

An American Airlines wide-body Airbus A300 on final approach to St. Martin. This island and its runway approach are a favorite for commercial-aviation enthusiasts. *Joe Towers/Check Six*

tors the aircraft's weight, the amount of fuel on board, the distance to be flown, the cruising altitude, and whether there is an altitude step involved in the flight plan. If the aircraft is initially too heavy to make it to the actual cruising altitude, the pilots can specify an attainable altitude for the first part of the flight, and then as the aircraft burns off fuel and gets to a lower weight, the FMS will call up and ask the pilots if they want to continue climbing up to a higher altitude or

not. The forecasted winds are entered—whether a headwind or tailwind will be encountered and its anticipated velocity. Using this information, the system will climb the aircraft in an optimum fashion. The FMS constantly monitors the engine pressure ratio (EPER) limitations and fuel flow, and using its own capabilities, the FMS will find out if there is indeed a headwind or a tailwind. Then, it will modify the climb or descent of the aircraft accordingly. At

altitude the FMS is programmed to minimize the movement of the throttles, and it will give plus-or-minus-100-foot altitude deviations to try to maintain a certain speed without moving the throttles. When the throttles are manually jockeyed back and forth, the engines burn more fuel. The FMS will also cue the pilots when to begin the descent. The system is programmed for an idle-power descent, descending from altitude at the last possible moment because jet engines are most efficient at high altitude. The system is designed to optimize the fuel burn, thereby keeping costs down.

The next item to check is the hydraulic manual out-flow valve that controls cabin pressurization. This is done by turning a large yellow wheel next to the captain's seat until it is locked down. Then, the pilot ratchets the wheel all the way forward before releasing it. This runs the valve through its full range of travel, making sure that cables from the cockpit to the valve are not binding. This manual two-valve system is used when the automatic pressurization system is in-operative and the flight crew has to run the pressurization. The valve controls airflow in and out of the cabin through use of the manual operating wheel in the cockpit. The flight would take off unpressurized, and then the pilots would slowly close the valve, located on the aft, port side of the DC-9 series, to increase pressurization as the aircraft gains altitude. After the larger of the two valves closes, a smaller one comes into play to adjust the cabin altitude when climbing or descending. When cruising at 37,000 feet, most aircraft fly with pressurization equivalent to that at 8,000 feet. To meet this optimum setting during a manual-pressurization flight, pilots must increase the cabin's pressure altitude 300 or 400 feet per minute on ascent and 700 feet per minute on descent. The plane is landed unpressurized to prevent the passengers ears' from popping and to enable the plug type doors to be opened.

After spinning the big wheel, the communications radios are checked, and the proper frequencies for the flight are set. The transponder, which provides altitude reporting and aircraft identification information to air traffic controllers, is tested next. The captain then checks the trim controls. These are run all the way through to their limit stops, ensuring that none of the cables are binding. Trim controls are then set to zero, or neutral, or what the captain thinks is appropriate for takeoff, thus completing the captain's pre-flight checklist.

The moment of touch-down. Here, a Cathay Pacific Boeing 777 touches down after a test flight prior to delivery. *Chad Slattery/Check Six*

Delta Boeing 757-232 N617DL (msn 22907) rolls out after landing. *Joe Towers/Check Six*

By this time, the first officer is back inside and he picks up the Automatic Terminal Information Service (ATIS—broadcast at each tower-controlled airport), giving the latest weather. The ATIS also gives the current local barometric pressure, which is set into the altimeter. Once this has been completed, both pilots run a cockpit pre-flight checklist. The first officer reads a challenge-and-response checklist. The captain checks the position or setting of a particular item and responds to the first officer.

Then, the paperwork is reviewed. Often weight-and-balance computations and performance figures are the responsibility of the first officer. Once this information is complete and logged on the

A Boeing 767 follows the "lead-in line" down the taxiway to the terminal area. *George Hall/Check Six*

"flight release," the captain reviews it, checking to see that the correct aircraft is listed, the proper flight-plan data is recorded, the fuel on board is enough for the flight, and the reserve fuel amount meets the legal minimums. If the captain feels more fuel is necessary, it can be quickly added. Weather at the destination airport and two alternate airports is also checked. Any items that are inoperative are listed on the flight release, and the captain checks to see that these do not affect the Minimum Equipment List (MEL). All items on the MEL or its backup equivalent must be functioning. Then, the pilot and

first officer discuss any special procedures that will be required because of the MEL (that is, if something is out, what will be done, and what different procedures will be necessary for this flight versus a flight on a "normal, everything operating properly" aircraft).

Once the captain is sure that the paperwork is correct, he signs it, along with the weight-and-balance, and waits to hand it to the station personnel. This is usually done just prior to shutting the door. About this time, the passengers are filing on. The flight attendants have already done their safety checks and

informed the cockpit crew of any known problems. Then, both pilots wait until the aircraft is boarded.

Where's the Beef?

While the flight attendants and cockpit crew perform their tasks, the aircraft is catered. Most airlines contract catering services to outside companies. Depending on the airline, this service

A Reno Air MD-90 climbs out of Long Beach, California. Captain Ed Cook flies an earlier model aircraft in the MD-80/-90 series. *McDonnell Douglas*

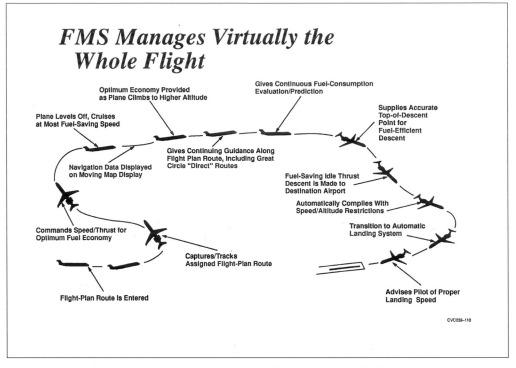

FMS Manages Virtually the Whole Flight

Optimum Economy Provided as Plane Climbs to Higher Altitude

Gives Continuous Fuel-Consumption Evaluation/Prediction

Plane Levels Off, Cruises at Most Fuel-Saving Speed

Supplies Accurate Top-of-Descent Point for Fuel-Efficient Descent

Navigation Data Displayed on Moving Map Display

Gives Continuing Guidance Along Flight Plan Route, Including Great Circle "Direct" Routes

Fuel-Saving Idle Thrust Descent Is Made to Destination Airport

Automatically Complies With Speed/Altitude Restrictions

Commands Speed/Thrust for Optimum Fuel Economy

Transition to Automatic Landing System

Captures/Tracks Assigned Flight-Plan Route

Flight-Plan Route Is Entered

Advises Pilot of Proper Landing Speed

CVC038-110

The FMS (Flight Management System) is used in all regimes of the flight. Using this computer, airlines can save millions of dollars in fuel costs, a savings that is often passed directly to travelers. *McDonnell Douglas*

A gorgeous in-flight study of a Cathay Pacific Boeing 777 turning shortly after takeoff. *Chad Slattery/Check Six*

All Aboard!

After passengers have been cleared to board by the gate agent, flight attendants are charged with ensuring that all carry-on bags have been securely stored and every passenger is seated and buckled in. Airlines have this down to a science, albeit sometimes an imperfect one. As soon as the gate agent calls for boarding, the airline gives flight attendants between 20 and 30 minutes to get everyone on board and seated. That is roughly 12–20 seconds per passenger!

During boarding, flight attendants make a number of announcements, including one checking to see that all passengers are traveling to the same destination as the flight. In theory, this has been double-checked by the gate agent, but one slips by occasionally.

While passengers board, the bags are loaded. They are separated in the cargo area, usually in three different sections. Most aircraft (727, 737, DC-9, MD-80/90 series, and larger aircraft use a containerized baggage system) have three "pits" in the front and three in the rear cargo holds. Luggage is separated by the handling that it requires—bags that are to be transferred at the next stop in one pit, and those traveling on to the destination city in the second. The third is used for overflow or intermediate stops.

After everyone has been seated, the gate agent brings the final paperwork to the lead flight attendant. This includes up-to-the-minute weather reports from flight dispatch, who the premium-class frequent flyers are and where they are sitting, any unaccompanied minors (children under 12), number of pet carriers stowed in the baggage compartment, and if anyone requires a wheelchair and their seat assignment.

The pilots hand their paperwork to the lead flight attendant, who passes it to the gate agent. Once the

Japan Airlines Boeing 777-246 JA8981 (msn 27364) passes Washington State's Mt. Rainier. *George Hall/Check Six*

can be simple, from soft drinks and peanuts, to hot meals and three-beverage services for 400 passengers. Catering trucks approach the loading door or doors. Specially equipped scissors-lift trucks elevate the cargo area of the truck, known as the "box," so that the box is even with the aircraft door's lower sill. Catering personnel insert safety railings between the box and the aircraft fuselage to prevent people from falling off. Then a metal bridge is placed between the door sill and the box, allowing carts to be rolled on and off the aircraft. Ovens and food trays are changed, drinks and ice are restocked, drinking water tanks on the aircraft are refilled, and trash cans are emptied and relined.

Colorado Springs-based Western Pacific Airlines leases the sides of its aircraft as flying billboards, known as LogoJets, for two-year periods. Boyd Gaming Corporation has adorned Boeing 737-301 N301AU (msn 23229) with an advertisement for the Stardust Casino. *George Hall/Check Six*

pilots clear the lead flight attendant to close the cabin door, another round of hustled activity begins.

Prior to and Push Back

Once the door is closed, flight attendants communicate that fact to the cockpit crew, acknowledging that the cabin is secured and ready for flight. The FARs require that each passenger be seated and buckled in before the aircraft is backed away from the gate. Flight attendants then perform the cabin walk-through, looking to see that each passenger has his or her seatbelt fastened, that any bags on the floor are stowed completely under the seat in front of the passenger (allowing free foot movement in case of an evacuation), and that all overhead bins are securely closed.

Having stowed all of the checked baggage, the ground crew closes up the airplane. After securing the belly cargo hatches, a walk-around inspection is completed, ensuring that all doors are properly closed and the handles secured, all flaps are sealed, and all panels are closed. The jetway is backed away from the fuselage, and the ground crew takes up positions off each wing.

One of the first aircraft to become a LogoJet was Boeing 737-301 N949WP (msn 23230). All of the animated characters of Fox TV's *The Simpsons* appear on the fuselage and tail of the aircraft. *George Hall/Check Six*

In the cockpit, the before-start checklist is performed to ensure that all doors and windows are closed and adequate brake pressure is available. The navigation lights and rotating beacons are then turned on and checked for proper operation. Depending on location, the aircraft will either be started at the gate and reversed with the aircraft's engines or be pushed back by another vehicle and the engines started and run up on the taxiway between terminals. After this has been determined, the first officer obtains clearance from the tower ground controller (known as "Ground") while the captain coordinates with the ground crew and flight attendants, who double-check to see that everyone is seated. Once Ground gives push-back permission and the flight attendants have responded, the captain releases the brakes and signals to the ground crew to back the aircraft away from the gate. The plane is rolled away from the terminal while the ground crew walks alongside the wings, ensuring clearance between other aircraft parked at neighboring gates.

After the aircraft has been pushed back and is positioned to taxi out, the tow bar is unhooked, and a

Boeing's 777 prototype cruises over the Pacific on a test flight. *George Hall/Check Six*

N375TA, a Boeing 737-3S3 (msn 23787), wears the colors of the Professional Rodeo Cowboys Association on the port side and has "Pro Rodeo Hall of Fame" and a different cowboy on the starboard tail. *George Hall/Check Six*

small pin in the landing gear is removed. This pin prevents the nose wheel from castering, giving better directional control to the tug driver. Once the pin has been removed, ground steering command of the aircraft is returned to the cockpit crew. When clear of the terminal area, the ground crew gives the captain a signal to start engines. The first officer starts the engines while the captain monitors what is going on. Once the engines are running, the captain obtains permission from Ground to taxi toward the runway. The ground crew then salutes, bidding the flight crew a safe journey.

Heading to the Runway

While the aircraft taxies out, the cabin crew performs the safety demonstration, or on larger aircraft, plays a videotape of the instructions. During the video presentations, flight attendants are required to stand at their assigned doors in case anyone has a question. Their presence near the exit doors while on an active taxiway is also mandated by the FARs.

En route to the runway, the rudder is exercised and the yoke is moved full travel in each direction (elevators up and down, looking to see that spoilers deploy and retract). On the DC-9 series, the aircraft is equipped with a powered elevator to assist in recovery from a deep stall. When the yoke is moved forward, the flight crew checks to see that this hydraulic system is working.

Then the flight crew performs another checklist, during which the first officer reads and responds to the captain's acknowledgments. Flaps and slats are acknowledged by both crew members as a triple check that they

El Al Israel Airlines currently operates two Boeing 737s, eight 757s, four 767s, and 13 747s including 4X-ELC, a 747-458 with 12 first-class seats, 42 business-class seats, and 424 economy-class seats. This aircraft was delivered to the carrier in May 1995. *George Hall/Check Six*

are in the takeoff position. Nearing the runway, radio frequencies are changed from Ground to tower flight controllers, or "Tower." The captain always taxies the aircraft on the ground but, depending on whose flight leg it is, may turn the aircraft over to the first officer for takeoff once lined up on the runway. Prior to lining up on the runway, the captain will make an announcement for the flight attendants to take their seats in preparation for takeoff.

Wheels Up!

After Tower gives takeoff clearance, the flight crew runs the power up to 1.4 EPER. (The EPER is the difference in pressure between the air coming in the front of the engine and that coming out of the back. This is a baseline number that establishes the engine's limitations. The EPER changes as the temperature and density altitude change. This is computed automatically and is presented to the flight crew on a gauge that has a changing limit that increases as the

aircraft gains in altitude and the temperature decreases. Some aircraft do not have this feature, but it is standard on those equipped with JT-8Ds. Some aircraft use the speed of the fan rather than EPER.) While this is done, both pilots monitor the engine gauges, ensuring that all engine parameters are within set guidelines. Once the engines are "spooled-up," the flight crew manually increases power to takeoff settings or commands the auto-throttles to perform this function.

Lockheed L-1011-385-1 TriStar N31009 (msn 1029) was delivered to Trans World Airlines (TWA) on May 16, 1973. The aircraft served until October 1992, when it was retired by TWA and placed into storage at Mojave, California. It was subsequently re-registered HR-AMC and was reportedly scrapped at Hurn, Bournemouth, Dorset, England, in August 1995. *George Hall/Check Six*

When the engines reach maximum takeoff power, the brakes are released and the jetliner starts down the runway. At 80 knots (92 miles per hour), the non-flying pilot calls out the speed and both pilots acknowledge, "Checked, 80 knots." Then, the non-flying pilot calls out "V1" (Velocity, One—this speed, depending on weight, is between 120 and 160 knots when the aircraft weighs 160,000 pounds maximum gross weight), which is the speed where an aircraft must take off and an abort cannot

safely be accomplished. When "V1" is called, the captain removes his hand from the throttles, eliminating any inclination to pull them back, thereby aborting the takeoff. At V1 there is not enough runway left to stop the airplane safely. Numerous accidents, including the loss of life and the aircraft, have resulted from aborted takeoffs after V1.

Shortly after V1, the non-flying pilot gives the "rotate" command. The flying pilot smoothly pulls back on the yoke, bringing the plane's nose up

about 3 degrees per second. Depending upon the airport, the rotation rate can be as high as 8 degrees per second. Once the aircraft lifts off the ground, a nose-up attitude of up to 20 degrees is set (climbs greater than 20 degrees are

NEXT: The bright colors of El Salvador's TACA International Airlines adorn the fuselage of Boeing 737-3Q8 N374TA (msn 26286). Powered by two CFM56-3B2 engines, this aircraft is configured to seat 136 passengers in all-economy class. *George Hall/Check Six*

Interesting underside view of Far Eastern Air Transport (FAT) Boeing 757-29J B-270007 (msn 27204). This aircraft was delivered in November 1994, and can carry 207 passengers in an all-economy-class seating arrangement. *George Hall/Check Six*

uncomfortable for passengers, especially nervous ones). As the aircraft leaves the ground, the non-flying pilot acknowledges that a positive rate of climb has been established, verified by the vertical-speed indicator. The flying pilot will then ask for the landing gear to be retracted. At 400 feet, "heading select" is called out, and the pilot will either continue the climb-out or prepare for the crosswind turn. When 1,000 feet is reached, pilots configure the aircraft for a cruise climb. This is done by reducing the vertical speed to half of its rate, then retracting the flaps and slats.

Once the climb has been established, Tower informs the non-flying pilot to change radio frequencies to departure control, or "Departure." Below 10,000 feet, large aircraft are restricted to a maximum speed of 250 knots. After reaching 10,000 feet, the crew performs the climb checklist to begin acceleration to the optimum

climbing airspeed. Flying through 18,000 feet, the non-flying pilot sets the altimeter at 29.92, or standard barometric pressure. When the departing aircraft reaches the end of the climb phase, Departure hands the flight over to the Air Route Control Center, or "Center."

Cruising Comfortably at 37,000 Feet

With the aircraft now cruising, both pilots monitor the aircraft's systems. If all is well, the pilots see that the cabin pressurization is operating as set, and they double-check fuel balance and whether it is being burned from the proper tanks. Navigation and communication duties occupy most of the cockpit crew's time during the cruise portion of the flight. Transmission from Center controllers advise the crew of any other air traffic in the aircraft's vicinity and also funnel flights into landing lines for the destination airports. If the air is clear at cruise, the

pilots will usually turn off the "Fasten Seatbelts" sign and make the announcement, "While in your seats, keep your seatbelts fastened." The pilots also announce estimated time of arrival and weather conditions at the destination.

Having established the cruise, the crew sends a departure message to the flight-dispatch office, providing them with time out of the gate and time of takeoff. With this information, the dispatchers determine the estimated time of arrival (ETA) at the destination airport.

While the flight is en route, the dispatcher is responsible for monitoring the weather. If anything unusual is reported, such as turbulence or thunderstorms, the dispatcher informs the flight by radio. Should something go wrong onboard the aircraft—for example, a loss of pressurization that forces the plane to travel at a lower altitude—the dispatcher must figure out if the flight will have enough fuel to continue on to its destination airport or if it should land and take on additional fuel before continuing the trip (jet engines consume higher quantities of fuel at lower altitudes).

Ten minutes after takeoff, flight attendants serving the coach, or rear section of the plane, start to set up the galley. They begin to cook the meals and prepare the beverage carts. Meals are delivered onto the plane cold in carts that both heat the entrees (using a heating pad) and at the same time cool the salads, desserts, and silverware with refrigerated air.

While the meals are being prepared, a couple of flight attendants will sell headsets for the in-flight movie.

Dispatcher Tom Birkley works for ATA (American Trans Air), and one of the carrier's Boeing 757s is seen here. Indianapolis-based ATA operates a fleet of more than 55 aircraft, including 757-23A N59AW (msn 25493). This aircraft has since been re-registered N512AT to reflect its new operator. *Chad Slattery/Check Six*

Once this task is completed, a full beverage service is provided. After the drink carts are clear, the meals are served, and the movie begins. Following the meal, a second beverage service is completed. Then the flight attendants pick up all of the empty cups and meal trays. Often, cold water will be served from trays about an hour after the meal service.

If the flight encounters turbulence and the pilots turn on the "Fasten Seatbelts" sign, by law the flight attendants must stop what they are doing and make sure that each passenger is buckled in. Turbulence can be severe enough that flight attendants must stop their service and take a seat until smoother air is found.

Descending to the Destination

In preparation for the descent, the non-flying pilot will get a report from ATIS for the destination airport. This report gives the crew an idea of the conditions upon arrival and what needs to be done to set up for the approach. The non-flying pilot will then take over control of the aircraft while the flying pilot reviews his approach plate before briefing the other pilot. They will discuss any abnormalities that will have to be dealt with, such as a missed approach (aborted landing), and what will be the alternate airports if the destination is fouled for some reason. The landing weight of the aircraft and the approach speeds for the aircraft are also reviewed. These numbers are listed on "speed cards" that quickly provide the crew with the proper speed at which to deploy slats, flaps, and spoilers. These numbers are plugged into the airspeed indicator as "bugs." These bugs give a visual reference to the non-flying pilot, prompting him or her when to call out an aircraft configuration change.

Control is transferred back to the flying pilot, and the non-flying pilot turns on the "Fasten Seatbelts" sign, usually as the aircraft passes through 18,000 feet on its descent. Once the sign is illuminated during descent, this lets

Boeing 757-2Y0 XA-KWK (msn 26151) flew with Transportes Aereos Ejecutivos (TAESA) from June 23, 1992, until April 27, 1995, when it was returned to the lessor, GE Capital Aviation Services. *George Hall/Check Six*

The volcanic peaks of eastern Washington State give the appearance that this TACA International Airlines Boeing 767-33A (ER, N768TA, msn 25535), is flying over some exotic location en route to its home base of San Salvador, El Salvador. This aircraft was returned to the lessor on October 14, 1994, and was subsequently leased to Vietnam Airlines and re-registered VH-NOE. *Chad Slattery/Check Six*

the cabin crew knows that it has roughly 20 minutes before landing. At about this time, radio guidance is passed from Center to "Approach" control.

Descending through 10,000 feet, the pilots slow the aircraft to 250 knots, and the approach controller vectors the flight onto a new heading for final approach. As the aircraft continually slows, deploying flaps and slats, Approach control sequences the flight in with other aircraft for landing. "Ideally, as the aircraft turns from base leg to final approach and the plane is being vectored in behind another aircraft, the plane should be slowed back to 170 knots, and flaps either 11 or 15 degrees in the DC-9/MD-80," said Captain Edward Cook. "If the weather is really bad, the captain will configure the air-

craft so that about a mile or two before the final approach fix, the landing configuration is set and all the pilots have to do is concentrate on the actual landing itself."

On a manual approach, as opposed to one using the auto-pilot, the pilot tracks the localizer and the glide slope on descent, and the first officer makes various calls through 1,000 feet—sink rate, speed, at 100 feet above minimums, and minimums. At minimums, the flying pilot makes the determination whether to continue the approach or to go around (executing a missed approach). If a go-around is initiated, Tower controllers will either give a heading or have the pilot fly the published missed-approach procedure on the instrument-approach plate. It works

Emirates Boeing 777-21H A6-EMD (msn 27247) first flew on May 2, 1996, and was delivered to the carrier on June 4, 1996. This airline intends to take delivery of an additional six aircraft by the end of September 1997. *George Hall/Check Six*

the same with the auto-pilot when shooting the approach. The decision height "is established by various parameters that are on the approach plate," said Captain Cook. "The first consideration is whether the whole system is working: Is the glide slope operational, are the approach lights in service? It can also be determined by the lack of current local weather information. If a flight was using weather from an airport a few miles down the road, the minimums would be increased.

"The best-case scenario for a Category IIIA approach is 700 feet runway visual range that is measured by a Transmissometer, a system that measures the transmission of light through the atmosphere. For our normal Category I approaches, it is 200 feet above the ground and one-half mile visibility. At some less-sophisticated airports, the minimums are higher."

When the captain makes the "flight attendants prepare for landing" announcement, landing is roughly 10 minutes away. At this point, the cabin crew should have all of its duties completed and equipment stored. The attendants then pass through the cabin to ensure that all seatbelts are fastened, tray tables and baggage are stowed, and seat backs are in the "full upright and locked position." Flight attendants then sit in their assigned jump seats until after the aircraft has rolled out upon landing.

Touch Down!

During the landing phase, the non-flying pilot will call out various items to the pilot, spreading the workload between the two professionals. As the jetliner touches down, the spoilers will automatically deploy, and the non-flying pilot will acknowledge this. If the

spoilers don't deploy, they must be activated manually. The spoilers disrupt airflow over the wing, reducing the lift, thereby shifting weight onto the wheels so that the brakes are more effective.

Once the aircraft is rolling along the runway, the pilots start the procedure to reverse thrust on the engines, which further slows the plane. The non-flying pilot will acknowledge when the reverser buckets are unlocked and deployed in the reverse position. Each engine has two thrust-reverser check lights—one yellow to indicate unlocked and one blue to indicate that the reverser buckets have deployed into position. The flying pilot listens to hear the non-flying pilot call "four lights," and at that point the flying pilot can add reverse thrust to the engines. Having used reverse thrust, the pilot begins to transition from reversers to wheel brakes. By the time the non-flying pilot calls out "60 knots," the reversers should be stowed to eliminate the chance of damage from foreign objects being sucked into the engines.

At 60 knots, if the first officer is flying, the captain will be on the rudder pedals and the tiller in preparation to take over command of the aircraft. When the captain calls out, "I've got the airplane," that transfers command from the co-pilot to the captain, who will slow the aircraft to either turn off onto a high-speed taxiway or continue the roll out and exit farther down the runway. As the aircraft clears the runway, the first officer assumes control of all radio communication while on the ground. The first officer will contact Ground to obtain the necessary instructions for taxiing in to the terminal.

When transitioning from the runway to the taxiway, the captain will retract the spoilers and ask the first officer to retract the flaps and begin the after-landing checklist. This checklist helps the cockpit crew ensure that the spoilers are retracted, the slats and flaps are stowed, and the indicator lights for these items are out. The checklist also calls for a decision to be made about the APU; will it be running during the layover or not? As the aircraft taxies in, getting close to the gate, the first officer lets the captain know what the brake pressure is—if it is in the green. If it is not, this is the time to take action—before turning and running into the gate.

As the aircraft nears the terminal, both pilots are watching for ground traffic. Catering trucks, vans, bag loaders, and tugs pulling trains of baggage carts all move quickly between aircraft and can be a hazard. The first officer is also in contact with company operations confirming the arrival-gate instructions for the captain.

Pulling into the gate area, the captain slows the plane down and turns onto the lead-on line. Marshalers walk the wings, ensuring clearance between aircraft parked at adjoining gates. They in turn feed clearance information by hand signals to the marshaler in visual contact with the pilots. Using hand signals the marshalers fine-tune the aircraft's approach to the gate and give the indication to stop by bringing their hands together in an upward motion. When the hands come together, the aircraft should stop. This stopping point is determined by stripes below the jetway, each indicating where the nose wheel for a certain aircraft type should be positioned.

Once the aircraft has come to a full and complete stop, the pilots engage the parking brake and turn off the "Fasten Seatbelts" sign. They then shut down the engines. Sometimes one engine may be kept running to provide cabin lighting until external power can be hooked into the aircraft, or both engines will be shut off, and the APU will be run to provide power.

The flight crew then reads through the after-parking checklist, ensuring that the parking brake is set, the engines are shut down, the "Fasten Seatbelts" sign is off, the anti-ice switches are off, and the fuel pumps are set up for the particular engine-off configuration (if the APU is running, one pump will be needed to supply it). Then, the first officer calls in the time the aircraft landed and was "blocked-in" at the gate, gives the fuel on board for the dispatcher, and the aircraft's status (whether it has items that need attention from the maintenance department).

Once the plane has come to a complete and full stop, the ground crew chocks the wheels and the nose gear pin is inserted. Then the tow bar is attached and the belly cargo doors are opened. At the same time, a jetway is positioned up to the first door to allow passengers to deplane.

In the cabin, the flight attendants disarm the emergency chute slides as the plane approaches the gate. It is an expensive proposition if a door is opened at the gate and the emergency slide deploys. Costs to repack the chute are upwards of $100,000.

Then starts the "200 bye-byes." While the passengers are deplaning, ground crews position belt loaders at the baggage hatches and the catering truck wheels up to the rear door. The bags, mail, and freight are removed and loaded onto carts. These are pulled by a tractor down to the bag room, where they are off-loaded onto belts that will carry them to the baggage carousel and waiting passengers. Freight and mail carts are then towed to the cargo facility.

A computer message is sent to flight dispatch giving the times for landing and into the gate, and the fuel remaining figure. Flights are required to carry a certain amount of reserve fuel and this is carefully monitored at the dispatch office.

If the dispatch office does not receive notice of "on and in times" within 30 minutes of a flight's estimated time of arrival, dispatch is required to find out what has happened. This is usually accomplished by a telephone call to the gate or a radio call to the plane. If more than 1 hour elapses without word from the flight, a company emergency must be declared and the airplane found. "Sometimes that gets interesting," said Tom Birkley. "A plane will just disappear in some of these third world countries. You can't get through by phone or fax, and its kind of scary sometimes. You think everything is OK, but you just don't know. I've had a few in Central Africa and South America particularly. They have terrible communication problems there. Planes will just disappear for 3–5 hours. We have no communication with them. That gets a little hectic sometimes."

If the aircraft has a long stop, ground power will be supplied rather than running the APU during the turn around. Usually on stops less than 1 hour, the APU is used.

Then the cycle begins all over again.

CHAPTER 3

THE END OF THE LINE—JETLINER BONEYARD

Mention the name "Marana," and visions of stored airliners come to mind, but aircraft storage is just one highly visible facet of the day-to-day operations of the Evergreen Air Center.

Located 30 miles north of Tucson, Arizona, the Evergreen Air Center occupies 2,200 acres on the site of the former Marana Army Air Field. Built in July 1942 for the US Army Air Forces, the site served as a basic-flight-training facility until the end of World War II. In 1948, the airfield and its buildings were deeded to Pinal County. The US Air Force maintained the facility for contracted flight-training operations until 1960. During the 1960s,

A line-up of engineless former-Continental Airlines Boeing 727s at Tucson, Arizona. *Nicholas A. Veronico/Airliners Magazine*

An aerial view showing Boeing 707s and 720s in storage at Davis-Monthan Air Force Base, Arizona. These aircraft contributed numerous parts for the KC-135E upgrade program. Some aircraft have undergone explosive tests to help in the fight against airborne terrorism. *Nicholas A. Veronico/Airliners Magazine*

Aerial view of the Evergreen Air Center, Marana, Arizona. The aircraft storage area totals 2,200 acres with 20 million square feet of paved ramp area. *Evergreen Air Center*

the field was run by Intermountain Aviation—a Central Intelligence Agency front corporation. When the US government pulled the plug on the intelligence agency's corporate ventures in the mid-1970s, Evergreen International of McMinnville, Oregon, purchased the assets of Intermountain.

Aircraft storage has always been a large part of Evergreen's operations at Marana. The air center is served by a 6,850-foot-long by 150-foot-wide lighted runway that is stressed to handle the largest wide-body jetliners. The field offers 20 million square feet of concrete ramp for aircraft storage that will accommodate almost 300 aircraft. The Evergreen Air Center offers two types of stor-

age programs—long term and short term. If an airline brings an aircraft to Evergreen and wants to store it for six months to a year, it is prepared for a long-term stay. That entails "pickling" the aircraft. In the pickling process, all windows are covered with a sprayed-on coating called "spraylat" to prevent ultraviolet rays from damaging the interior, all orifices on the aircraft are sealed to prevent entry by water or pests, and all gear boxes are lubricated and filled with oil to remove air from the space. Depending on the aircraft's size, it takes anywhere from one to three days to prepare it for "deep storage." The cost of long-term storage ranges from $250 to $1,000 per month, depending on aircraft type.

For a stay up to six months, a short-term or flyable storage program is adopted. Every 28 days the aircraft is pulled out and the engines, gear boxes, and systems are run and the tires are rotated. An aircraft can be removed from short-term storage and be ready for flight within 12 hours. This method is the most expensive way to store an aircraft, and is nearly equal in cost to flying the aircraft because the maintenance requirements are the same for a flying aircraft as for one in short-term storage.

Although aircraft storage is the backbone of Evergreen Air Center's daily operations, times are changing. Trends in the aviation industry within the last two to three years have seen

The main hangar at Evergreen Air Center can handle any size aircraft. Here a former Air Canada Lockheed L-1011 is being returned to service for a new carrier. *Evergreen Air Center*

Here, Boeing 747 N471EV (msn 20652) is being prepared for its new operator Saudia—Saudi Arabian Airlines. *Evergreen Air Center*

Cockpit sections are all that remain of two former Pan Am 747-121s. Delivered in April 1970, N749PA (msn 19653) and N750PA (msn 19654), originally *Clipper Intrepid* and *Clipper Rambler*, respectively, were reduced to spare parts by the end of 1992. *Nicholas A. Veronico*/Airliners *Magazine*

more and more aircraft returning to flight status. Near the end of the 1980s, hundreds of aircraft were in storage in the United States alone, but as new carriers enter the market and established carriers require additional aircraft, fewer and fewer jetliners are being "mothballed" and many that had been in long-term storage have been refurbished to reenter service. This has lessened the demand for the company's storage services while increasing its aircraft maintenance and service operations. The air center holds an FAA Unlimited Repair

This line-up of Boeing 727s is headed by USAir's N747US. A 727-281 (msn 20569), it was originally delivered to All Nippon Airways as JA8339. The plane then flew for Piedmont as N866N *City of Denver* and was re-registered N747US shortly before Piedmont merged with USAir. The tri-jet is believed to have been scrapped. *Nicholas A. Veronico*/Airliners *Magazine*

Airbus Industrie A300B4-203 N202PA (msn 195) basks in the Arizona sunshine after Pan Am's demise. This aircraft was subsequently acquired by Sempati Air of Indonesia and re-registered PK-JIC. This A300 is configured for 24 first-class and 230 economy-class seats *Nicholas A. Veronico/Airliners Magazine*

Station license, giving the company authority to complete all major modifications and checks, and strip paint. Any modification or repair can be made to any airplane from the smallest all the way up to a 747-400.

"We have found that this segment of our business is increasing," said Dave Fowler, president of Evergreen Air Center. "There are several aspects to that. One is the airline industry is flying older aircraft longer because of economical situations in the industry, and secondly,

Boeing and McDonnell Douglas are trimming back the delivery dates, but that is changing. The third factor is that there are some repair stations on the West Coast that have gone out of business."

Evergreen is capable of putting an aircraft through a complete "D" check—which is the rebirth of an aircraft. A D check is the heaviest check that can be performed on a jetliner. It occurs every 6-10 years during an aircraft's life. The D check entails totally inspecting the aircraft from the ground

up. "A" checks are the simplest, usually done on line. "B" checks are a little heavier, requiring about three to four days to complete. The B check involves opening certain inspection panels on the wings and fuselages, changing oils and filters, performing light maintenance, and completing Deferred Maintenance Items (DMIs). Tires, wheels, and brakes are also serviced during the B check. "C" checks take from 14 to 30 days to complete, depending on the specified level of the check. For example, Boeing has C-

A ramp view of the rear storage area. An Airbus, four DC-10s, and a half dozen Grumman Albatross amphibians await new operators. The Airbus A310-203 in the foreground, PH-MCA (msn 281), was last operated by KLM Royal Dutch Airlines before its arrival at Marana. The jetliner has been converted to freighter configuration and is now operated by FedEx as N423FE. *Nicholas A. Veronico/*Airliners *Magazine*

1 through C-6 checks, C-6 being the most thorough. Evergreen is also authorized to effect Section 41 checks on 747s, change landing gear, and make engine pylon modifications (remove the engine and pylon from the wing, perform the modification, and reinstall the assembly onto the wing). These items are usually performed during the D check or under special maintenance directives from the FAA or the manufacturer.

Everything on an airplane has a rated lifespan that is expressed in terms of the number of hours, or the amount of time it has been in service (calendar days). An item is only governed by one system. After a predetermined number of hours has passed, the subject part must be removed and sent to an authorized overhaul facility where it is inspected, overhauled, certified flight ready, and returned for reinstallation. Landing gear is a good example–it can only be operated, or landed upon, so many times (cycles), and then it must be removed from the plane and inspected. If it fails to meet the specified tolerances and can not be certified flight ready, the item is scrapped and new unit must be installed.

The Evergreen Air Center employs about 300 full-time workers. Aside from aircraft maintenance and storage, Evergreen has an on-site avionics shop capable of servicing Class I, II, III, and IV avionics. They maintain, overhaul, and remanufacture black boxes—voice and data recorders, weather radar, and almost all of the avionics in DC-8s, DC-9s, 707s, 727s, and 747s.

An interior fabric shop handles all insulating work, seat covering, and modifications. For example, if a customer wants a 747 reconfigured from a three-class interior (first, business, and economy) to a two-class (first and economy), Evergreen's shops are capable of removing the business-class seats, and installing additional economy-class seats. This modification also involves redesigning and reconfiguring the aircraft's interior—moving galleys, restrooms, overhead bins, and partitions. Evergreen's shops can also strip out an interior, plug the windows, and reinforce the floors, thereby converting a passenger-carrying jetliner into a freighter.

The air center also boasts a survival- and emergency-equipment shop and a component overhaul shop for hydraulic, pneumatic, and mechanical accessories; a sheet metal shop; and a non-destructive testing (NDT) lab. Evergreen does light work with composite materials but prefers to subcontract such work to more cost-effective suppliers. Evergreen works on Quick Engine Changes (QECs —complete, ready to hang engine accessory sections; the engine is installed into the QEC and then hung on the aircraft), but they do not repair the hot or cold sections of the engines or rebuild engines.

The company also works closely with the Central Arizona College and Pima College's aviation programs by giving freshly trained airframe and powerplant mechanics (A&Ps) summer jobs providing hands-on experience. It works both ways: Evergreen gets well-educated, eager men and women ready to work, and journeymen mechanics earn money to help with their college tuition.

Stripping and Painting

Evergreen Air Center has made a capital investment in a stripping and painting facility that can handle jetliners as large as the 747-400.

There are many ways to strip an aircraft—by using chemical strippers or by blasting with various media such as glass or plastic beads or small pellets made from walnut husks that are propelled by high-pressure air—but most of those methods eventually do damage. Anytime a medium is blown at an aircraft's skin under high pressure, it will eventually distort or erode the metal, so this manner can only be used a limited number of

Clipper Beacon Light, a 747-123 N9674 (msn 20326), was modified with a side cargo door to 747-123(SCD) configuration and awaits a new buyer. *Nicholas A. Veronico/Airliners Magazine*

Evergre
Boeing
liners M

in cas
appoi
the su
tions
many
askin
be gr
anyth

the n
Airpe
Some
the p
conti
infor
ager

Ang
loca
nam
moc

This Convair 440-86 N442JM (msn 438) was originally delivered to Eastern Air Lines on July 22, 1957, as N9320. After a 13-year career at Eastern, it was re-registered and began a new life flying for a number of smaller airlines. It is seen in storage at Avra Valley in July 1993. *Nicholas A. Veronico/ Airliners Magazine*

A Convair 440 N442JM, a former-military Convair C-131 N43944, and a Fairchild C-119 Flying Boxcar N175ML represent some of the diverse aircraft types parked in storage yards across the United States. N175ML was recently flown from Avra Valley and donated to the Mid-Atlantic Air Museum, Reading, Pennsylvania. *Nicholas A. Veronico/Airliners Magazine*

Sports teams make up a large part of the large-jet charter market. The Los Angeles Dodgers have operated a number of aircraft, including Boeing 720-023 (msn 18022), seen in storage at Davis-Monthan Air Force Base, Arizona, where it was stripped of parts for the KC-135E program. *Nicholas A. Veronico/Airliners Magazine*

An aerial view showing Boeing 707s and 720s in storage at Davis-Monthan Air Force Base, Arizona. These aircraft contributed numerous parts for the KC-135E upgrade program. Some aircraft have undergone explosive tests to help in the fight against airborne terrorism. *Nicholas A. Veronico/*Airliners *Magazine*

Aircraft from the fleets of TWA, American, and Tradewinds Airlines can be seen in this aerial view of Davis-Monthan Air Force Base. *Nicholas A. Veronico*

Boeing 707-123B N701PC (msn 17639) last flew for Denver-based charter carrier Ports Of Call. This aircraft was originally delivered to American Airlines as N7512A, *Flagship Pennsylvania*, on May 21, 1959. *Nicholas A. Veronico/*Airliners *Magazine*

Boeing 737-222 N9033U (msn 19071) *City of Memphis* was the 85th of its type down the assembly line, and was delivered to United Air Lines on October 23, 1968. It had nearly a 24-year career flying the "Friendly Skies" before being sold to International Aviation Support Company of Tucson, Arizona, on June 24, 1992. *City of Memphis* is being broken up to supply other flying 737s with parts. *Nicholas A. Veronico/*Airliners *Magazine*

Aircraft are stored, leased, and operated, and then returned to storage to await the next contract. Here, Lockheed 188C Electra N107DH (msn 2013) is seen at Hamilton Aircraft, Tucson, Arizona, after it was leased to Transcarga in July 1993 and three years later, after its titles had been painted out. *Nicholas A. Veronico/*Airliners *Magazine*

Still going strong! This Buffalo Airways DC-4 (C-54G-15-DO, former-USAF 45-0635, msn 36088) is seen at Hamilton Aviation after major repairs were completed to the lower nose section after its gear collapsed. *Nicholas A. Veronico/Airliners Magazine*

Boeing 727-2B7 HI-612-CA (msn 20302), named *Luperon*, was leased by Dominicana de Aviacion of Santo Domingo, Dominican Republic, for a short period in the early 1990s. It is seen in July 1993, shortly after its return to International Air Leases. The aircraft was subsequently broken up for parts. *Nicholas A. Veronico/Airliners Magazine*

Sometimes the colors of a forgotten airline will turn up on an aircraft in storage. Douglas DC-9-14 N931EA (msn 45698), the fifth DC-9 built, had returned to storage only 12 days before this picture was taken in July 1993. In March 1994, msn 45698 was leased to Mexican carrier Allegro Air and re-registered XA-SPA. *Nicholas A. Veronico/Airliners Magazine*

Boeing 727-214 (msn 20162) prepares to begin an eight-month lease with Mexican carrier Allegro Air, wearing its new registration XA-SJM. *Nicholas A. Veronico/*Airliners *Magazine*

Boeing 727-63 N3720 (msn 19846) is seen in storage at Mojave on December 1, 1989, in the colors of Boeing/GE after its work on the Un-Ducted Fan (UDF) project. *W. B. Slate*

Originally delivered to Northeast Airlines, then having served with Delta, Boeing 727-295 (msn 20249) was acquired by Pan Am on November 11, 1983. Pan Am re-registered it N372PA and christened it *Clipper Onward*. By the time the plane was photographed in May 1996, it been retired to the boneyard, where it had been stripped of almost all of its useable parts, including landing gear, doors, windows, engines, and tail feathers. *Nicholas A. Veronico/*Airliners *Magazine*

Grumman G.159 Gulfstream I N39TG (msn 39) was part of Purolator Courier Corporation's fleet before being withdrawn from use and stored at Mojave. It was subsequently sold to Drenair on February 7, 1990. *W. B. Slate*

Boeing 707-436 G-APFF (msn 17707) was delivered to British Overseas Airways Corporation on May 13, 1960. After a 17-year career, the aircraft was placed into storage, and was later traded into Boeing for new aircraft. It met the scrapper's torch at Kingman, Arizona, in 1981. Only the fuselage remained on December 13, 1982. *W. B. Slate*

Originally delivered to Northeast Airlines, then having served with Delta, Boeing 727-295 (msn 20249) was acquired by Pan Am on November 11, 1983. Pan Am re-registered it N372PA and christened it *Clipper Onward*. By the time the plane was photographed in May 1996, it been retired to the boneyard, where it had been stripped of almost all of its useable parts, including landing gear, doors, windows, engines, and tail feathers. *Nicholas A. Veronico/Airliners Magazine*

Grumman G.159 Gulfstream I N39TG (msn 39) was part of Purolator Courier Corporation's fleet before being withdrawn from use and stored at Mojave. It was subsequently sold to Drenair on February 7, 1990. *W. B. Slate*

Boeing 707-436 G-APFF (msn 17707) was delivered to British Overseas Airways Corporation on May 13, 1960. After a 17-year career, the aircraft was placed into storage, and was later traded into Boeing for new aircraft. It met the scrapper's torch at Kingman, Arizona, in 1981. Only the fuselage remained on December 13, 1982. *W. B. Slate*

Boeing 727-63 N3720 (msn 19846) is seen in storage at Mojave on December 1, 1989, in the colors of Boeing/GE after its work on the Un-Ducted Fan (UDF) project. *W. B. Slate*

CHAPTER 4

JETLINER PHOTOGRAPHY— HOW THE PROS DO IT

How often do you see airline commercials on TV showing jetliner flying to some exotic location or banking off into the sunset? What about slick magazine ads with an air-to-air photo of a jetliner with the advertising type set around it? As a result of such slick shots, the reader or viewer is often enticed into purchasing that exotic vacation or traveling to see friends and family. But where do airlines get those great photos and film clips that so effectively sell the excitement of flying and air travel?

Air-to-air cinematography was in its infancy in the 1920s and 1930s with films such as *Wings* (Paramount, 1927) and

Cinematographer Doug Allen manipulates the controls of the Astrovision system. The small Hi-8 video recorder and screen above the unit provides Allen with a color copy of the footage shot. If necessary, upon landing, he can use this video to give clients an idea of what was shot. Assistant Scott Smith monitors the amount of film shot. *George Hall/Check Six*

Airbus A300 (A300B4-605R) N11060 (msn 470) was delivered to American Airlines on October 13, 1988. It is configured to seat 16 in first class and 251 in economy class. *George Hall/Check Six*

One of the first and most colorful of Western Pacific's LogoJets is Fox Television's *The Simpsons* featuring the characters (from left to right/tail to nose) Marge, Bart, Homer, Maggie, and Lisa. *George Hall/Check Six*

The majority of the approach and landing photographs are shot at Moses Lake, Washington, a field Boeing maintains for crew training. In this airspace the Lear Jet can safely follow a subject aircraft, here an Air India 747-400, through its "touch-and-go"—approach, landing, roll-out, and takeoff. *George Hall/Check Six*

The pilot's seat is an excellent vantage point from which to shoot still photos. Photographing above the cloud layer will provide the airline with footage and stills with a universal background. KLM 747-406 (SCD) PH-BFO (msn 25413) is equipped with a side cargo door and was delivered to the carrier on October 8, 1992, wearing the name *City of Ottawa*. *George Hall/Check Six*

Howard Hughes' epic *Hell's Angels* (United Artists-Hughes, 1930). A number of advances in aerial photography were made during World War II, but it was the sale of thousands of war-surplus aircraft that led aerial stunt pilot Paul Mantz to modify a North American B-25 Mitchell bomber into the period's ultimate air-to-air camera ship. Clay Lacy then took aerial cinematography into the jet age with his first modified Lear Jet in the early 1960s. Today, his company, Clay Lacy Aviation of Van Nuys, California, is the most widely known and respected of those providing specialized air-to-air camera platforms.

Born in 1932 at Wichita, Kansas, Lacy took an early interest in aviation. His first professional flying job was with United Air Lines, a company he would later retire from in August 1992. During the Korean War, he joined the US Air Force and later flew C-97s, T-33s, and F-86s with the California Air National Guard. He went on to set a number of aviation records and notable feats, including being the pilot on the first flight of the heavily modified Boeing 377PG "Pregnant Guppy"; winning the National Championship Air Races Unlimited Class flying his purple P-51D Mustang *Snoopy* at an average speed of 307.342 miles per hour; finishing sixth out of a field of 33 air racers at the 1970 California 1000 while flying a Douglas DC-7; setting a round-the-world speed record of 36 hours, 54 minutes in 1988 at the controls of the United Boeing 747SP *Friendship One*, which raised more than $500,000 for Children's Charities of the World; and setting a number of records flying a Gulfstream IISP equipped with Aviation Partners' Blended Winglet System in November 1996.

Lacy's Lears and the Astrovision System

In 1974, the Astrovision system was built by Continental Camera, also of Van Nuys. John Carrol, president of Continental Camera, contacted Lacy because the latter was already providing a Lear Jet camera platform to the entertainment industry. At the time, Lacy's jet was using

mercial aircraft. Allen, like Hall, is an experienced pilot and cinematographer. "I made all of Lear Jet's films for a 10-year period between 1972 and '82," Allen said. "I had heard of the Astrovision system and I knew Lacy, so I asked him to come back to Wichita in 1975 and shoot some air to air of a flight we were making. Not knowing that Lacy brought cameraman David Nowell to operate the system, I hopped in the seat and started using it. Much to Lacy's amazement, I was pretty good at it. Over the years, it has gotten to the point that Nowell films all of the Hollywood movies that require a union cameraman, and I'll do the non-union work. Over the last 20 years, I have become second cameraman on the system and have shot most of the work for Boeing, McDonnell Douglas, and for individual airlines.

"My dad took 16-millimeter movies beginning in 1924, so I sort of grew up with a camera in my hand. After graduating from Stanford, I went into the Navy and flew SNJs, T-28s, and then S2Fs with VS-37 for four years. After getting out, I decided I wanted to go back to business school and get my master's degree. During that time I started working with a fellow who was producing movies for the university. I received an immense amount of training in movie production from him.

"Shortly thereafter, I received a Nuffield Foundation grant and joined that group's Unit For The History of Ideas. Nuffield was a philosopher and author on the development of Western thought and science. The Unit For The History of Ideas had talked the foundation into making a series of books and motion pictures on the growth of Western thought, science, and technology. I

It is hard enough to fly formation with the Lear Jet and a subject aircraft. Multiply the difficulties by three when two Condor 767-330 (ER [extended range]) jetliners are led by a Boeing 757-230 during a June 1991 photo shoot. This was one of the hardest shoots for George Hall. Each aircraft must be spaced perfectly, as evidenced here. *George Hall/Check Six*

After Clay Lacy retired from United Airlines, he stepped from the captains seat of a Boeing 747 to the left seat of his Douglas DC-3/C-47 N541GA (msn 34370). This aircraft was built too late to see service in World War II and spent the majority of its life as an executive transport. *George Hall/Check Six*

777-246 JA8981 (msn 27364), named *Sirius*, was the 23rd of its type down the assembly line. Japan Air Lines is calling its 777-200s "Star Jets" and plans to christen each aircraft with the name of a constellation. *George Hall/Check Six*

was with them for one year and worked with the Shell film unit, British Film Institute, the Slade School of Art at London University, and learned an awful lot about motion pictures.

"After earning my MBA, I bought an Arriflex camera and started producing motion pictures for anyone who would give me the opportunity. First, I worked for Stanford, then the Stanford Linear Accelerator Center

[SLAC]. Because of my interest in aircraft, I leaned toward working on documentaries, marketing films, and corporate capability films in aviation. As I went along, mostly by word of mouth, I made films for Hiller, Evergreen Helicopters, Intermountain Aviation — which later became Sierra Pacific Airlines—then Harry Combs of Lear Jet liked my work, and he put me under contract to produce films for them. Then

Linden Blue, who had become assistant to the president at Lear Jet, asked me to make movies for him at Lear Fan. When he went to Beechcraft as CEO, he asked me to make movies there, which I did

N31009 (msn 1029), a Lockheed L-1011-385-1 TriStar 1, passes over San Francisco's Golden Gate Bridge. One of the first airfields in the state, Crissy Field, can be seen to the left of the bridge tower. *George Hall/Check Six*

Boeing 727-2B7 Advanced N772AL (msn 22164) was delivered to USAir on May 5, 1981. After passing through a couple of owners, the aircraft was re-registered OB-1590 and currently flies for Aero Peru. It is configured to seat 12 in first class and 128 in economy class. *George Hall/Check Six*

for four years. During all of these times, we would use Lacy and the Astrovision system to document the first flights of aircraft, such as the Lear Fan, the Lear Jet 55, and many others."

Shooting the Giants of the Sky

Airliner air-to-airs are usually done on a test flight. Flight B-1 is the aircraft's maiden flight while B-2 is its second test flight. For Boeing aircraft, ground and approach shots are filmed at Moses Lake, Washington, and transoceanic scenes are captured out over Straits of Juan de Fuca, off the northern coast of Washington State's Olympic Penninsula.

Since air-to-air photography is an expensive proposition, all of the footage must be shot in one or two consecutive flights. Each trip is tasked with committing certain shots to film that are accomplished through a standard set of nearly 50 maneuvers developed by Lacy and Allen over the years. Because the lenses have a fixed focal length and cannot zoom, the subject aircraft flies a constant heading and Lacy uses the Lear as a camera dolly. Allen explained: "All of the maneuvers are usually done by us. The subject plane has the lead and we are flying off of them. We prefer that they just fly straight and level on autopilot. In

all of the scenes where the subject aircraft looks like it's moving, in actuality we are moving in relationship to the subject. The aircraft does the dollying and the subject remains in the same location." Some of the maneuvers have the Lear fly into the scene with the camera holding on the nose, or flying through 90 degrees. From numerous TV commercials comes the easily recognizable "fly-in hold on the logo," the "start on the tail and let the airplane drift forward," and the "start on the tail logo and fly forward getting the whole aircraft" maneuvers. Lacy also performs 360-degree fly-arounds of the subject aircraft, as well as

DeHavilland DHC-8-102 Dash 8 N811PH (msn 023), named *Great City of Seattle/Tacoma*, is one of 23 operated by Horizon Air in the Northwestern United States, feeding Alaska Airlines. *George Hall/Check Six*

a number of passes in front from right to left and back; then they pass in back left to right and right to left. Since the Lear is equipped with both an upper and lower camera, frequently these manouvers are flown twice.

"Then we have what we call our 'Star Wars' shot in which we get below and aft of the subject plane and let him fly forward over us," Allen continued. "We are limited by the endurance of the airplane. The photo shoots are done under 18,000 feet, below the minimum altitude of positive air traffic control. This gives us more freedom of what maneuvers we can accomplish. But, below 18,000 feet, flying

a Lear Jet with CJ-610 engines, it consumes fuel fast, so we have a maximum time in the air of 2 1/2 hours. We will frequently drop down, land, and refuel while the jetliner orbits the field at altitude. In 15 or 20 minutes we can fill the tanks and climb up to begin shooting again. On occasion, we will go up into positive control to get shots of the jets making contrails. I have talked Lacy into getting up pretty high when I wanted pictures of Lear Jets simulating flight at 51,000 feet—up where the sky turns Royal Blue approaching black. Some of the Lear Jet films I made had that quality when the planes were contrailing.

"I like early morning light when the sun is high enough to be front-lit on the subject aircraft. Right at sunrise you only get silhouettes. Our lowest f-stop is f6.3 so we cannot work in very, very low light conditions. The sun has to be up above the horizon before enough light is falling on the surface of an aircraft for us to really expose it well. And that depends on the film stock. My favorite is 5293, which is equal to 125 ASA, and it has a lot of latitude. I prefer not to change the exposure in mid-pass—especially when you consider that we are working all around an aircraft. We will shoot dark side to light side all the time.

Clay Lacy set a 36-hour, 54-minute around-the-world speed record in this 747SP-21 N147UA (msn 21548), christened *Friendship One*, in January 1988. This record-setting flight raised more than $500,000 for Children's Charities of the World. *Roger Ritchie*

Rather than change the exposure while filming, it can be manipulated in post-production editing during the film-to-videotape transfer. I will leave the exposure where it will underexpose on the bright side, and over-expose on the dark side. The 5293 film stock has the latitude of one f-stop over or under. I try to balance it so that everything can be gleaned out of the negative that you possibly can."

Motion picture film is shot at 24 frames per second (fps) and TV is shot at 29.94 fps. When converting from film to video, there is virtually no loss of picture quality. Allen usually shoots at 24 fps, but a producer for Cathay Pacific prefers his film shot at 64 fps. That

Clay Lacy in the left seat of the Lear near Colorado Springs, flying formation on a Western Pacific "Sam's Town" LogoJet. Note the TV monitor mounted on the glare shield. This gives Lacy a simultaneous video feed from the periscope cameras, enabling him to "dolly" the aircraft for the perfect shot. *George Hall/Check Six*

Up close and personal. Lacy tucks the Lear's wing in tight on an Alaska Boeing 737. This shot conveys just how close the aircraft are when shooting air-to-air. *George Hall/Check Six*

speed gives more detail per frame. Reportedly, most car commercials are shot at 64 fps. Because of the slower aperture speed (1/125 of a second) at 64 fps versus 24 fps (at 1/50 of a second), each frame is sharper.

Getting the Shots on Film

The subject for this air-to-air photo shoot is British Midland's new 737-300 G-ECAS (manufacturer's serial number [msn] 28554). This aircraft made its first flight November 21, 1996, and was delivered to the airline on December 16 of that year. British Midland is leasing this plane from General

Electric (GE) Capital Aviation Services. Currently, the carrier has 25 Boeing 737s in its fleet and typically operates its 737-300s configured to seat 131 passengers.

The first 737-100 was rolled out of the Boeing factory on January 17, 1967. The second-generation 737, the -300, was rolled out 17 years later on January 17, 1984, and first flew February 24, 1984. This aircraft type is the best-selling jetliner of all time, with more than 3,300 of all variants sold and more than 2,700 having been delivered as of June 30, 1996. Approximately 250 air carriers operate the 737 in 95 countries.

G-ECAS was rolled from Seattle's Boeing Field paint hangar December 9, 1996, at 11 A.M., as the participants were headed to the pilot's briefing. Flying British Midland's newest acquisition will be James C. "Jim" McRoberts, Boeing's chief experimental test pilot, and Richard A. "Randy" Austin, senior production test pilot. Also in the briefing is Clay Lacy, cinematographer Doug Allen, and still photographer George Hall. Lacy, McRoberts, and Austin have flown air-to-air missions hundreds of times, so the briefing is professional, yet relaxed. Each knows and respects the other's skills, plus they have all previously flown

121

Preparing for a photo shoot: A Westjet Boeing 737-275 Advanced C-GWJE (20588) taxies out as the Lear crew gets ready to start engines. *George Hall/Check Six*

JA8977 (msn 27636), a Boeing 777-289, was the first of three delivered to JAS. The "Rainbow Seven" scheme wraps around the fuselage from nose to tail. This aircraft made its first flight on October 23, 1996, and was delivered to the carrier on December 3 of that year. *George Hall/Check Six*

formation together. Air speed is set at 250 knots, filming will be done at 16,500 feet (below positive air traffic control, which starts at 18,000 feet), and the subject aircraft will be flown on autopilot. The aircraft will file and fly an Instrument Flight Rules (IFR) departure to IFR on top of a layer of low clouds. Any banks or breakaway maneuvers will be hand-flown, not to exceed 40 degrees of bank.

Next, the afternoon's weather is discussed. A front is moving in, currently off the west coast of Washington State. This information helps the pilots decide to film over the water to the west in an attempt to use that area's background features before the front comes to shore. Secondary film-ing areas, preferably locations that will match scenery flown over by British Midland, are selected and briefed.

A list of the maneuvers the subject pilots can expect the Lear Jet to perform are then reviewed. Film of the air-craft with the landing gear extended has been requested by the airline, and landing gear extension speeds are given to Lacy.

Once the briefing has ended, the crews depart for their respective air-planes. Both aircraft are scheduled to depart at 2 P.M., filming to last until 4:15 P.M., nearly sunset at this time of year.

After the crew is onboard the camera plane, N564CL, a Lear 25, Lacy takes the right seat and will fly acting as the film's director. Sitting behind the cockpit bulkhead is still photographer George Hall, and on the other side of the camera turrets is camera assistant Kelly Diehl. Seated against the rear bulkhead, facing the camera control console is cin-ematographer Doug Allen. He sits on the port side, with the starboard seat avail-able for a producer or airline marketing director, who may fly along to observe or to obtain a particular shot. Allen's con-sole features fast/slow tilt control, pan speed control, a black-and-white 10-inch screen, and a camera control joy stick. Mounted above the console is a Hi-8 video recorder and color monitor. This gives Allen a video that can be shown to manufacturer or airline representatives waiting on the ground to see the results of the film shoot.

After the pilots have pre-flighted the aircraft, Diehl and Allen triple-check the camera system. Prior to takeoff, nitro-gen is used to blow out the periscope tubes, upper and lower, to remove any condensation that has formed. Light read-ings are taken. Filters are chosen and set, and then both cameras are loaded.

The Lear taxis out for takeoff ahead of the 737. After takeoff and climb to altitude, the 737 joins up with the Lear, and photography begins as the two jets headed toward Victoria, on the southern end of Vancouver Island, British Columbia, Canada. Lacy, watching his glare-shield-mounted video screen, flies the aircraft and simultaneously gives instructions to Allen as he films, "Pan, pan, hold it. Pan, pan, slow, slow, stop." Allen acknowledges with, "Cut," as Diehl checks the film-exposed counter on the camera.

After the film crew has gotten its shot, Lacy gives Hall the go-ahead to shoot. Hall asks for angles above or below and positions ahead or behind while Lacy quickly positions the jet for the right still shot.

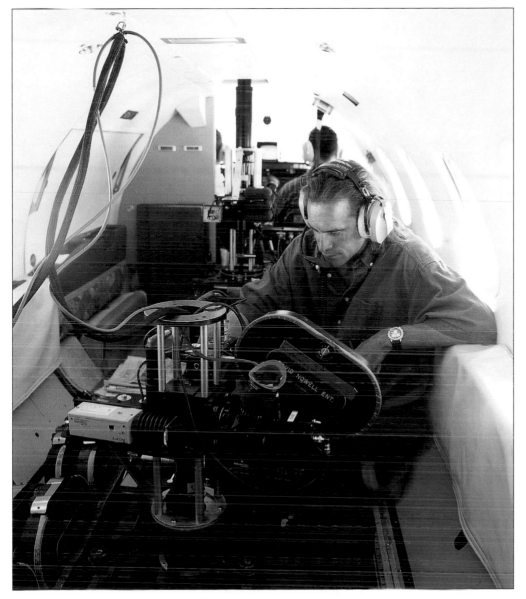

Scott Smith keeps an eye on the Astrovision system. Only the lower camera was installed for this shoot. *George Hall/Check Six*

British Midland Boeing 737-36N G-ECAS (msn 28554) first flew on November 21, 1996. These photos were shot December 9, hours after the plane rolled from the paint hangar. G-ECAS was delivered to British Midland seven days after this air-to-air photo session. The airline currently operates 23 examples of the 737. *George Hall/Check Six*

Light-meter readings are taken, and Allen requests Diehl to adjust for a different aperture setting on the periscope barrel, and filming begins again on Lacy's command. After the segment is shot, Diehl changes the film magazine by rotating the camera and removing the cartridge. The area is dusted with high pressure air, and a new film magazine is installed. While filming is under way again, Diehl puts the cartridge into a light-proof bag before removing the exposed footage from the cartridge and sealing it into a film can—all done by feel. The can is removed from the light-proof bag, and its lid is securely taped down and tagged with color-coded tape. "We usually have between 17 and 24 film cans, each 4 minutes in length," Allen said. "About 45 minutes of film is exposed per shoot. I shoot a lot. I'm sort of the brunt of the jokes about heavy-handed shooting fingers, but I figure that if the camera is not on, you're not going to get the picture if something interesting happens. I'd rather shoot too much than too little."

A number of maneuvers are completed, and the process is repeated. Lacy gives the directions, Allen films, Diehl works in an incredibly tight space, and Hall shoot pictures and

KLM 747-406 (SCD) PH-BFO (msn 25413), christened *City of Ottawa*, is perfectly lit by the late-afternoon sun. The diverse topographical features of Washington State provide fantastic photographic backgrounds. *George Hall/Check Six*

dodges the whirling camera turrets, awaiting his turn to shoot.

As the sun dips closer to the horizon, Lacy, Allen, and Hall concentrate on getting a shot of the sun shining through the cabin windows of G-ECAS. It is a standard shot they try for when flying close to sunset. After three or four agonizingly close tries, the maneuver is accomplished and everyone is satisfied with the shots taken. Lacy and Allen first did this maneuver with a Pacific Southwest Air-

lines (PSA) aircraft in the late 1970s. "It is getting harder and harder because windows are continually getting smaller and airplanes are getting bigger and bigger with more in them," Allen said.

As darkness closes over the Pacific Northwest, the Lear and the British Midland 737 break off and head for Boeing Field. Just over 2 hours of flight time, nearly all of the movie film exposed, and Hall with some outstanding stills, earns the crew a hearty "mission accomplished."

"Soar to meet your Destiny" is Colorado Tech's motto. An eagle with outstretched wings brings it to life. Western Pacific's N952WP, a Boeing 737-3B7 (msn 23378), was acquired by the carrier in July 1995 and is configured for 138 passengers in all-economy seating. *George Hall/Check Six*

This is the type of photograph an airline's advertising art director dreams of—Garuda Indonesia Boeing 737-4U3 PK-GWL (msn 25714) bathed in golden sunlight. Beautiful work such as this has earned George Hall his outstanding reputation for high-quality air-to-air photographs. *George Hall/Check Six*

The first 737-484 delivered to Greek carrier Olympic Airways was SX-BKA (msn 25313). Arriving in September 1991, this colorful 737-400 is powered by two CFM56-3C1 engines and seats 150 passengers. *George Hall/Check Six*

Malaysia Boeing 747-4H6 9M-MHO (msn 25126), named *Alor Setar*, crosses the threshold at Moses Lake, Washington. Hall's 80-millimeter lens does not truly give an indication of how close the Lear is to the 747-400. *George Hall/Check Six*

Icelandair Boeing 757-28A TF-FIK (msn 26276), named *Soldis*, looks as if it's cruising between Reykjavik and Keflavik. Captured over the Cascade Mountains shortly after its first flight, on March 7, 1996, it was delivered to the carrier on March 15. *George Hall/Check Six*

ATR42-312 N421MQ (msn 014) was acquired by American Eagle in June 1986. This aircraft seats 46 and is operated by Simmons Airlines as a feeder for American Airlines. *George Hall/Check Six*

Air Canada adopted a new paint scheme, and Boeing 747-133 C-FTOC (msn 20015) was one of the first to display it. This photo has been seen in numerous display ads and aviation calendars. *George Hall/Check Six*

A three-ship formation of two Condor 767s led by a 757. All three aircraft were delivered simultaneously to the German airline. *George Hall/Check Six*

Boeing 747-4F6 N751PR (msn 27261) of Philippine Airlines was delivered in November 1993. This aircraft is leased from Wilmington Trust Company. The winglets carry a duplicate of the tail logo. *George Hall/Check Six*

This Air Berlin Boeing 737-46J, D-ABAH (msn 27826), first flew January 27, 1995, and was delivered on February 8. This 400-series 737 is configured to seat 167 passengers. *George Hall/Check Six*

The boom in the overnight-freight and small-package business has kept many first generation jets in the air. Re-engined to meet strict noise standards and to improve performance, McDonnell Douglas DC-8-73F (AF) N796FT (msn 46104) will fly well into the next century. *George Hall/Check Six*

Chilean carrier Ladeco operates a pair of Boeing 757-2Q8s, including CC-CYG (msn 25044). This aircraft serves alongside the airline's fleet of early 727s and 737s and a wide-body A300B4-203. *George Hall/Check Six*

Garuda Indonesia also operates the Boeing 747-400. PK-GSG (msn 25704) was photographed prior to its trans-Pacific delivery flight in January 1994. Garuda has configured its 747-4U3s to seat 18 in first class, 64 in business class, and 323 in economy class. *George Hall/Check Six*

Virgin Atlantic Airways operates three 400-series 747s. G-VFAB (msn 24958), christened *Lady Penelope*, was delivered to the carrier on April 28, 1994, and entered service May 19, 1994. *George Hall/Check Six*

Passing over the coast, Clay Lacy rolls the Lear Jet up as this TAESA 757 banks to the right. Unusual attitudes and interesting backgrounds draw viewers into the photograph. Notice how the coastline does not detract from the subject aircraft, yet it subtly shows movement. *George Hall/Check Six*

Although they represent only a fraction of the photos that are delivered to the customer airline, these four shots are a good representation: side views, a trailing shot, close-ups, and photos over famous landmarks, in this case the Sydney Harbor and Opera House. Clay Lacy ferried his camera-equipped Lear to Australia specifically for this shoot. *George Hall/Check Six*

Nicaraguenses de Aviacion (NICA) leases this Boeing 737-2T5 Advanced N501NG (msn 22395). The aircraft was delivered to the Latin American carrier June 24, 1992, and was christened *Momotombo*. *George Hall/Check Six*

This Western Pacific Boeing 737-3Q8, N956WP (msn 24299), is the second LogoJet to be adorned in "Sam's Town" colors. Its sister ship, N955WP, wears the same scheme, only with different showgirls on the each side of its tail. *George Hall/Check Six*

A DC-10 flight arrives during a fantastic sunset. Imagine the view while the aircraft was at altitude. *Sam Sargent/Check Six*

"I have a shot that has made me more money than any I've ever taken," said George Hall. This is it—a head-on takeoff shot of a USAir Boeing 737. "We were shooting the plane for the airline at Akron, Ohio, early one Sunday morning. We had the airport closed for an hour and were out on the runway having the pilot fly right at us." *George Hall/Check Six*

BIBLIOGRAPHY

Books

Derogee, Erik, Paul Simon, and Peter van Stelle. *Airlines & Airports, Coding & Decoding*. Woerden, The Netherlands: EPS Aviation Productions, 1994.

Eastwood, A. B. and J. Roach. *Piston Engine Airliner Production List*. West Drayton, Middlessex, England: The Aviation Hobby Shop, 1991.

Klee, Ulrich (chief editor). *JP Airline-Fleets International 96/97*. Zurich, Switzerland: Bucher & Co., 1996.

Roach, J. R. and A. B. Eastwood. *Jet Airliner Production List*. West Drayton, Middlessex, England: The Aviation Hobby Shop, 1992.

———*Turbo Prop Airliner Production List*. West Drayton, Middlessex, England: The Aviation Hobby Shop, 1994.

Periodicals

Airliners: The World's Airline Magazine. Various issues.

Airways: A Global Review of Commercial Flight. Various issues.

World Airline Fleets News. Various issues.

INDEX